£5 ~
ARr
1X40

ENGLAND'S PLEASANT LAND

Vision & Reality

Take not too much of the land,
weare not out all the fatness,
but leave it in some heart.

Pliny the Elder, AD 23–79

FRONTISPIECE: *May morning in Gloucestershire.*

ENGLAND'S PLEASANT LAND

Vision & Reality

Anthony Rosen
with paintings by David Mynett

QUILLER PRESS
LONDON

First published in 1988 by
Quiller Press Limited
46 Lillie Road
London SW6 1PN

Text copyright © Anthony Rosen 1988
Illustrations copyright © David Mynett 1988

ISBN 0 907621 95 3

Designed and produced by Hugh Tempest-Radford Book Producers
Printed in Great Britain by Purnell Book Production Limited

Contents

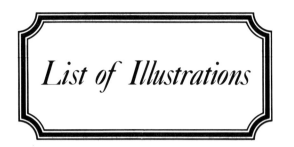

List of Illustrations

List of Illustrations

Dorset Farmland

Foreword

Lord Plumb of Coleshill

The future of our rural communities is a matter of increasing concern to the general public and the terms of the debate have become wide and varied.

This book gives a very clear picture of the struggle and progress through the ages to keep the countryside of England a truly pleasant land. It makes good reading for all countrymen and farmers providing a unique, beautifully illustrated and compelling study of rural development and the changing role of the family of the land.

This is also an important book for urban dwellers. It is essential that they understand and accept the ways of the countryside, particularly now, as the development of countryside culture and crafts is on the increase. The land must be seen and respected as the farmers' factory floor. An untidy or uncultured countryside is an unpleasant sight and, just as for industry, a policy which neglected the arts and sciences of farming would be a policy of national folly.

We are reminded that there are roughly the same number of people living in rural areas as live in London. Fourteen million cars are daily moving through England's pleasant land. This is creating heavy demands for more rural facilities in the next few decades. Such demands can only increase substantially in the future. We must all be prepared to fulfil these demands in the interest of the future prosperity of our countryside.

From a rural England that nearly lapsed into dereliction between the two world wars, when vast areas of land were abandoned to scrub, weeds and rabbits, we have become commercial exporters of food and have added £2.5 billion to our positive balance of trade. But farmers have become victims of their own success, a development which our fathers and forefathers would only have described as unbelievable.

New techniques, new plant varieties and new breeds of livestock have made possible the mass production of food. This is a comparatively recent development. As scientific and technical knowledge and applications have multiplied, so the farmer has been able to feed an ever greater amount of people. From the late nineteen seventies, this revolution in farming has started to work against the ordinary farmer.

In today's circumstances it has become very difficult for the farmer to plan ahead, to maximise income from every enterprise, to integrate properly every resource—whether managerial, financial, legal or physical. But the centre must hold: the farmer in his farm. This is the vital human resource.

Reducing surpluses and maintaining prosperity is one thing,

but maintaining a rural population in our villages is quite another. David Mynett's pictures and Anthony Rosen's writing show that they recognise this and offer several good options for the diversification of land. We have all become much more environmentally sensitive in the past few years, and David and Anthony correctly give prominence to these concerns. The effects of Chernobyl were certainly a stark reminder of the sensitive balance that exists between man and his environment. There is still scope for a considerable increase in woodlands. Alternative crops for energy production may well be a potential for development. Organic farming is growing rapidly and consumers are now becoming much more discerning in their food purchases. We ignore at our peril the consumer and conservation lobbies which outnumber farmers by twenty-five to one.

We need a stability plan and it has to be a long-term stability plan. The management and husbandry of the land is by nature a long-term business and once farmers know what nature can deliver and what politicians will expect, they will plan accordingly.

They will meet the hard challenge of change and they will make certain that England remains a green pleasant land. They will do that with vision and a sense of reality.

As a son of the soil and as a Midlander I could not sum up my views better than the comments in this book on the sunset over Warwickshire. But I should add a favourite description:

One of the first astronauts, Charles M. Duke, said in 1972 while in orbit around the Earth, 'The earth is the most beautiful sight in space, with all its colours of land and sea and clouds. Looking at it against the blackness of space was almost a religious experience for me.'

The land will always provide life and sustenance: we should never forget this, whether as large or small farmers, politicians, tradesmen or consumers. If England's pleasant land stops being a working land, then it will become derelict and useless. England cannot afford this to happen.

Introduction

THE unique landscape of England has been sculpted by generations of landowners and farmers.

Periods of prosperity over many centuries have allowed the English countryside to develop and to mature at a steady pace. No invaders have had to be repelled for over a thousand years, and, since the time of Cromwell in the seventeenth century, England has enjoyed internal peace—with no pillaging of land or wilful destruction of buildings. The farming community has, however, always been aware of the need for change and the countryside has evolved through a continuing pressure upon farmers to meet the changing needs of the nation.

Over the years many generations of wealthy Englishmen have put down roots in the countryside, buying and improving land, building large houses, creating spectacular landscapes and making a major contribution to the beauty of our land.

Nowadays, the development of the motorway network has spread commuting distance further from the cities and, as a result, villages in the countryside are becoming dormitories for the towns and cities. Many villages are changing dramatically to meet the different needs of their inhabitants. Some of the changes, such as the refurbishing of the houses and the general air of prosperity brought about by the injection of capital, are beneficial. Others, such as the closing of the village school and the demise of many of the local shops, are not.

Farmers and the rural community in the 1980s are accepting the need for change. With the vast mountains of surplus foods in Europe it is clear that the production of such foods cannot remain the first priority for all available farm land. Alternative land uses have to be found.

A Devon Village: Many farmers in Devon are happy to see the many millions of tourists who, in the months of July and August, descend upon this picturesque county with its narrow, high-banked lanes, but they can be seriously inconvenienced by the constant traffic when going about their daily tasks. Another problem facing those who farm in this popular tourist area is that of controlling those who visit their farms. Generally the visitors respond well to guidance and try to appreciate the farmers' point of view. But since Devon has over five thousand three hundred sheep farms (this means that sheep outnumber local residents by nearly two to one) the need for educating visitors in taking great care in the countryside is especially important—by shutting gates, controlling dogs, not leaving potentially dangerous litter about, etc.

The majority of farmers have over the years shown themselves to be responsible and caring guardians of the countryside and very responsive to the exhortations of their various governments. Indeed it is because of their response to continual demands by governments for greater and greater home food production, encouraged by guaranteed government-funded subsidies, that their present predicament has come about: too much food is being produced for current market needs.

If the nation really does want less home grown food and if the government is confident that a tragedy of Chernobyl proportions was a unique experience, and that a conventional war, with sea routes blockaded, is a thing of the past, then accurate forecasting of the nation's food needs can be assessed and England's farmers will respond accordingly.

Nothing could be worse for the farming industry's confidence than the uncertainty and indecision of the European Community over the past three years. When the governments of Europe decide how much of Europe's farmland must be taken out of food production, and over what period, then our farmers will know what steps to take and when to take them.

Forestry will flourish. New activities in the countryside will materialise to cater for the growing demand from urban dwellers for more and better leisure pursuits. Country sports will grow in significance and popularity with the greater recreation time available to our citizens. Rural industries will be encouraged.

The speed and the spread of change in these diverse directions will influence the changing panorama of the English countryside. The vision and reality of Rural England are in danger of becoming ever further apart.

Anthony Rosen

A Warwickshire Village: The difficult lands of the English midlands have always been a challenge to the skill of the local farmers. Much of the heavy clay land, ploughed for comparatively low yielding cereal production, is now returning to its original use—that is, to provide grazing land for beef and sheep. Farmers in these difficult land areas are realising the benefits of opening up their farms to the paying public by laying farm trails and providing viewing facilities if they have intensive livestock or indeed any livestock within buildings. Young animals are, of course, a big draw.

Warwickshire has both Stratford-upon-Avon and Warwick, towns which attract many visitors, especially from overseas. Local farmers are realising the 'honey-pot' effect of these two towns and are beginning to sell the attractions of the local countryside to the tourists.

MANY years ago, when I was a student at Agricultural College, during a winter evening lecture on 'Capital in Farming' and having created a diversion, the discussion turned to aesthetics in agriculture and the lecturer, the Principal of the College, George Jackson, now the Agricultural Director of the Royal Agricultural Society of England, remarked that he could not understand why no painter ever portrayed modern farming. At that stage I was not an artist—I was having enough trouble struggling to learn the rudiments of agriculture—but a diversion is a diversion and so I took up the argument. . . . 'because there is more pictorial romance in a sower walking the seedbed or a team of horses ploughing than in modern machinery'. As I started to work for this book I realised I was about to be hoist with my own petard.

How was I going to portray tractors and machinery in the field without making them a series of technical drawings and yet make them accurate? I am primarily a painter interested in the interplay of light and colour between the clouds and the landscape but any ideas I might have had of portraying tractors in the middle distance obscured by a belt of rain were sharply corrected by the Quiller Press and Anthony Rosen. 'You must make the farmer feel he is there,' they said. So I bethought myself. The answer I found in observation is that in reality tractors and machinery seldom dominate the landscape, they are part of it, reflecting and being influenced by light in the same way as horses or oxen. This gave me the theme for the book, that although the paintings are fixed in time, in the late 1980's (how different tractors will look in twenty years time, even the cattle will have a different profile in a hundred years), there is a unity with the past, namely the domination of nature over our efforts.

Water Meadows: In times past most water meadows were capable of being routinely flooded by a complex system of open ditches and drains. Well managed meadows were capable of carrying heavy stocking as well as providing a home for much welcome flora and fauna, but to yield their maximum in dry spells regular flooding was necessary. The cost of maintaining these ditches became too high as labour costs rose relative to farmers' incomes, and the need to use tractors for fieldworking added to the complications: also the skills of the 'watermen' have now virtually disappeared. Consequently over the past twenty-five years many thousands of acres of water meadow have been ploughed up and sown with cereals.

It is true that today farmers have more power to wound the earth, given methods presented to them by optimistic scientists. It is true, too, that today farmers have, unfairly, a less than perfect image among the public (Britain only really appreciates her farmers during a crisis). Yet the countryside has never looked so healthy or been cared for so well.

These thoughts I wished to portray in my illustrations; an age-old communion with the land, different from the past yet still as deeply felt.

Many of the illustrations were painted on the spot, while some were worked up in the studio afterwards. I hope that I have produced a balance between finished works and spontaneous reactions.

In the course of the work for this book I have met many farmers, land agents, landowners, Ministry and County Council employees and have enjoyed much hospitality. With unfailing courtesy and at times amusement, they have watched my efforts to depict their daily life. I have tried to portray the splendour and nobility of their work; their relationship with the animal and natural world is of immense importance in our modern more urban society. But, also, I hope I have shown the drudgery, the back breaking labour, the dedication needed to produce food for the country. I hope that one can see, for example, in the illustration 'milking time' what a hard task the dairyman will have washing udders before milking.

One hears a lot about the 'Agricultural Industry' but I wonder whether it is an industry; it certainly isn't called that in Europe. In industry it is easy and is indeed the aim to quantify substances and to measure exactly . . . in farming? How can one quantify a cow's happiness and yet it might be vital to milk yields. The cow's happiness or a wet August are factors that even modern scientists cannot master; though perhaps the urban housewife may be forgiven for not realising this when she sees the well stocked and packaged goods on sale at her local supermarket.

It has been an honour for me to illustrate this book and also a fascinating education to see, at close quarters, so many different aspects of food production. Not that it didn't have its difficult moments. A Lincolnshire landowner stopped the work, in the middle of harvest, in the field to let me draw and paint

The Yorkshire Moors: Littondale is one of the many dales in Yorkshire which provides a hardy type of living for the dedicated Dalesman. Many of the farmers have modernised their farmhouses and converted their outbuildings to provide very reasonably priced accommodation for the welcome tourist, who brings much needed revenue into the area.

Sheep farmers in the Dales are very quickly realising the benefit of housing their sheep through the winter months thus eliminating the losses that occur so often during heavy snowfalls. Not only do the sheep thrive better when protected from the extremes of the Dales weather but management is easier for the shepherd.

Even today, with the trend for sons of Dalesmen to seek a supposedly easier life in the towns or farming the lower land, many of the Dales farms do pass down in-hand from generation to generation.

the machinery—the sky was threatening—an awful feeling: suppose the sketch wasn't successful? Again, on a January pre dawn going to draw a milking parlour—the lights of the parlour shone invitingly, but alas, in the darkness between me and the lights was a large herd of enthusiastic Friesians. I had forgotten to bring a torch—I arrived considerably the worse for wear.

The most nerve-racking picture to paint was the portrait of the turkey stags, every time I picked up a pastel the entire barn gobbled. I finished the picture emotionally exhausted, with the determination never ever to become a turkey farmer. Other pictures appealed to my love of history, the Longhorn herd on a spring dawn by a medieval church was irresistible, and it was a pure delight to paint the East Sussex ploughing competition. It was such a perfect morning watching the vintage tractors ploughing and painting the scene accompanied by the evocative sound of the ploughman's commands to the shire horse teams.

Inevitably there are many omissions, some involuntary, some deliberate—a worm farm on a cold winter morning did not inspire me. I permitted myself a mild 'artistic fit' and refused—to all worm farmers and particularly to my host I apologise.

It has been a pleasure to work with the Quiller Press and Anthony Rosen. He is a journalist whose forceful arguments and provocative wit have led to many open discussions during the past decade among the farming community. Perhaps the comment of a nineteenth-century Czech historian, Frantisek Palacky, on the subject of the Austrian Empire, 'if it did not exist it would have to be invented', could equally well be applied to Anthony Rosen's journalism. However, as much as I admire the quickness of his thought on his more controversial themes, I don't *always* agree with his conclusions.

My pictures are not controversial but I hope that they reflect the present way in which our 'daily bread' is produced.

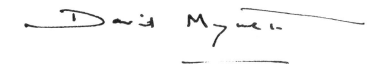

The Dorset Coast: This is a typical coastal landscape near Lyme Bay; it is mainly grassland, grazed here by Friesian heifers. The proximity to the sea largely prevents frosts and so the grass will come into growth sooner than usual in the spring and provide good early grazing for livestock as well as continuing to produce good forage for livestock well into the autumn. The damage that livestock, especially cattle, can do to pastures in wet weather, even those overlying the chalk soils of Dorset, means that the visitor to the countryside will see few animals grazing between December and March. Many farmers have converted traditional Dorset barns into well equipped buildings for over-wintering livestock thus enabling many of the arduous routine tasks connected with the keeping of animals to be done with a tractor rather than by hand.

The Land

SOON after the Second World War the Ministry of Agriculture carried out a land survey of Great Britain (which took twenty-five years) and then divided the quality of the twenty-five million acres of farmland in England into five categories, taking into account climate, topography and soil type.

Grade 1 is the best and is described in the official Ministry of Agriculture survey as being 'land with very minor or no physical limitations to agricultural use. The soils are deep, well drained loams, sandy loams, silt loams or peat, lying on level sites or gentle slopes and are easily cultivated'. But sadly only 3.3 per cent of the farmland in England can be classified as Grade 1 and 16.7 per cent Grade 2.

Grade 2 land is very similar to the best land (Grade 1) but with minor limitations which will exclude it from Grade 1—

usually to do with the soil, perhaps its texture, depth or drainage but occasionally due to minor climatic or site conditions, such as exposure or slope.

The largest soil type category of land in England is Grade 3, accounting for 54 per cent of England's total farmland area.

The greatest weakness in this system of land classification is the wide variation within Grade 3; the difference between the best and the worst land classified as Grade 3 is much greater than the difference between the best Grade 3 and Grade 2. Grade 3 land will have limitations on the range of cropping possibilities: only the less demanding horticultural crops such as brussels sprouts, cabbages and broad beans, can be grown.

Arable crops are limited to forage crops, while grass and cereals will be the predominant crops and the upper half of this grade will be able to produce reasonably good yields. Some

The Fens: The deep black soils of the Fens are capable of growing maximum yields of almost every crop planted. Whatever happens to farmland prices the Fenland soils of Grade I quality classification will always sell at a premium. Rental values on these fertile soils are also significantly higher because of cropping flexibility and the much higher yields and quality that are attainable.

The Fenman of times past learnt the skill of land reclamation from the Dutch who had had literally hundreds of years experience of claiming top quality soils from the sea. Today land reclamation continues around the coast of England, especially in Lincolnshire, but farmers make certain that they do not deprive wildlife of their habitats by making provision for them beyond the new dykes.

Good Fenland, when properly handled, can be used to grow two crops of vegetables a year.

of the best quality grassland will come in this grade where the other physical characteristics of the land make arable cropping inadvisable.

Grade 4 accounts for 15.7 per cent of England's farmland, and is aptly described as having severe limitations due to adverse soil, relief or climate, or a combination of the three. For example, land over six hundred feet above sea level which has over fifty inches of annual rainfall will always be graded 4 or 5. Land in Grade 4 is only suitable for low output enterprises: most of it will be under grass with occasional plantings of oats, barley or forage crops.

Grade 5 land, which accounts for 10.3 per cent of the country's farmland, has very severe limitations including adverse soil, steep slopes, excessive rainfall and exposure, usually very poor drainage, a shallow depth of soil and often excessive stoniness. All land above one thousand feet with over sixty inches of annual rainfall will be Grade 5, where only grass or rough grazing survive. More than half the 825,000 acres of Grade 1 land is in the eastern half of England with Cambridgeshire, Lincolnshire and Humberside being the most favoured—and Kent following close behind.

Historically, throughout the world, original land-settlers understandably chose the best land upon which to establish their towns and so over the centuries it is this best land which has been taken for housing and has thus been lost to farming for ever.

But now, since Grade 1 and Grade 2 land, of which only five million acres remain in England, is so superior in agricultural terms, it is to be applauded that recent planning legislation protects this vital part of our farming heritage from building development. Recent changes in planning laws have meant that the agricultural value of other land does not have to be taken into account when considering development applications.

The cynic maintains that England does not have a climate, only weather, but in fact England suffers far less than most countries from inclement weather conditions. Seldom does England have an extreme drought—the drought of 1976 was the worst for a hundred years with many parts of the country having less than eight inches of rainfall against a normal twenty-five inches during the nine months of the drought. Nor

A Dorset Village: Dorset is considered by many to be the most beautiful county in England. Unusually it is still largely owned by a few landowning families who have been there for generations. Because of the resulting scarcity of farms on the market and because many people desire to live in this lovely county the few farms that do come up for sale sell at a premium way beyond their straight commercial agricultural value. Even the steeper slopes of Dorset are heavily stocked and well farmed.

Oil exploration and nuclear power have spoilt small areas of the county but fortunately not excessively so up to the present time.

does England suffer from extremes of cold or excessive rainfall, or hurricanes—the night of October 16th 1987 excepted—which farmers have to contend with in so many agricultural areas of the world.

Many parts of England have an average yearly rainfall of thirty inches, spread evenly throughout the year, although generally (but it is dangerous to generalise when describing the weather) the months of January, September, November and December are traditionally reckoned to be the wettest and February, March and April the dryest.

The hurricane of 1987 in the south-east quarter of England destroyed over twenty million trees and damaged millions of others: it decimated orchards and destroyed greenhouses, buildings and houses, and changed the face of many areas. Gradually the fallen and damaged trees were cleared, and now the memory of the disaster is but a salutary reminder of the power of the wind. Had the hurricane struck during the day, and perhaps in July when the crops were ready for harvesting, the damage to humans, animals and crops would have been much greater—quite devastating, in fact, and one very good reason why stocks of basic foods should always be available.

But the comparatively reasonable weather in England ensures a reliable estimate of yields and it is seldom that such predictions are too far wrong. Because of the regularity of the rainfall irrigation is not generally considered essential and less than ten per cent of the country is equipped with any form of artificial watering system. These systems are mainly used for high-value crops, such as potatoes and other horticulture.

Because of the great variations in the weather and the topography of the land, the length of the growing season will vary across the country from less than two hundred days a year in the uplands of Yorkshire to over three hundred and twenty-five days on the Cornish peninsular: this variation is obviously another influence on the cropping in the different areas.

*

The forty-six million inhabitants of England have an average of just under three-quarters of an acre each in which to live. This average, however, hides a wide diversity and includes some boroughs of London with a density of nearly fifty people to every acre, while fortunately there are still some rural areas

Devon Landscape: In David Mynett's picture the hilly grassland, heavily grazed by sheep, gives way in the background to the bleak and difficult land of Exmoor. Whereas six ewes may well be kept to the acre on good grass-land, Exmoor itself provides little sustenance for livestock and they have to graze extensively to find enough nourishment. Many sheep are lost in the annual snowfalls on the moor.

Devon farmers are meeting pressures on their financial margins by developing alternative ways of utilising their resources. During the summer months the tourist trade brings in much needed revenue. Other than this any scope for alternative land-use is limited to improving their game shooting facilities and either letting the shoot or 'selling guns', which actually means charging keen sportsmen for a day's shooting.

with more than ten acres for every inhabitant. There are now about eleven million people living in England's rural areas, the same number of inhabitants as in London.

The new orbital motorway, the 117-mile M25 which encircles London, encloses nearly one million acres in which there is a resident population of nearly fourteen million people. Although there are still about 150,000 acres of land being used for farming within this concrete circle, one wonders whether, within our lifetime, all the farming land will have become urbanised or commercialised, with only pockets of green areas. Apart from a few small areas of very good Grade 1 land the majority of the farms and small holdings are poor Grade 3 and well suited to change of use.

There will continue to be many parks, paddocks and large gardens, but the growth of the commuter syndrome fuelled by the continuing move out of the city centres will inevitably mean that the planners will accept the need for even more dormitory towns and villages within the M25 circle.

There is the increasing availability of both public and private transport and thus the ability for city dwellers to travel long distances relatively easily. The recent electrification of the railways now means, for example, that the two-hundred-mile journey from York to London can be travelled in under two hours, while Norwich to London takes just ninety minutes for the hundred and fifteen miles—and the people of England own fourteen million cars.

Then, as road building improves and train journeys shorten in time the pressures on the countryside will also increase, especially as the improvement in working conditions for urban dwellers allows greater time for country pursuits—but they will still demand leisure activities close at hand.

Thus, within the M25 some of the land will be taken up by city farms open to the public, golf courses, leisure walks, parks and amenity woodlands, as well, of course, as with the ubiquitous horseyculture. (It is to be hoped that the horseyculturists will quickly come to realise what a dreadful eyesore many of their paddocks are, but surely they need not be?)

Exmoor: The dramatic and harsh climate on Exmoor (in Devon and Somerset) provides farmers with a challenge that becomes more difficult to meet as the squeeze on their incomes intensifies. A large area of Exmoor is over one thousand feet above sea level with steep ravines and many boggy areas. Land improvement is difficult and very expensive but in spite of these handicaps there are many farmers on Exmoor who would not want to farm elsewhere.

The grazing season on the moor is very short with the native grasses yielding almost nothing until the ground warms up in late May and after it goes into its winter dormancy in September. Grassland improvement on the moor has been tried with varying degrees of success, but the limited increase in stocking seldom justify the costs, especially now when there is little profit in extensive farming of sheep or cattle.

The continuing change in the age structure of the English populace will influence the way in which pressures on rural life will alter. The percentage of children under the age of fifteen is constantly falling—down to the present ten million—and rural schools are closing at a frightening rate. At the other end of the scale, the number of people who are over sixty-five is showing a constant increase, growing at nearly one per cent a year, with over nine million people in this age group at the moment (of these over three million are over seventy-five and half a million over eighty-five).

The wish of an increasing number of retired people to move to rural areas is putting additional demand on available housing. As an indication of this trend, for the first time in recent history both East Anglia and Yorkshire are showing greater percentage gains in rural house prices (although of course houses in these areas are still very much cheaper in absolute terms) than in most other areas.

With pressure from both the retired and the commuters, the rural planning authorities must release more land for sensible and well planned housing development.

In some areas the local councils have welcomed the changing composition of the villages. Indeed the South West England Business Development magazine declared 'Commuters give life to villages. Where once there were agricultural workers and local craftsmen, there are now accountants, doctors, solicitors and stockbrokers. This transformation is bringing prosperity to the region: discover life changing for the better.'

Farmers accept this continual need for change in the countryside and are constantly adjusting to it: all they ask is that the newcomers in their turn accept that the countryside is the farmers' 'factory floor' and that they respect the ways and the lore of rural life. Farmers accept and are proud of their social responsibility to care for the nation's heritage, which, of course, includes the conservation of the countryside: they have obligations as well as rights.

There is a lot of truth in the saying 'a good farmer is the one who lives as though he is going to die tomorrow but farms as though he is going to live for ever'.

A Cotswold Landscape: Over recent years there has been a strong tendency for more land in the Cotswolds to be cultivated for grain growing, but the real beauty of the Cotswold area lies in its grass fields with contentedly grazing animals. The very high ground that is found across most of the Cotswold area means that there is a strong tendency for long spells of bitter weather in the winters, often with very late springs and early autumns.

Many of the Cotswold stone village houses have been bought as second homes by weekenders who will spend their weekdays working in London, Birmingham or Bristol. The ubiquitous car and the ever improving motorway networks mean that villages that hum with life at the weekends are unnaturally dormant during the week.

Farming

THE claim that this country is one of the most efficient farming nations in the world has been made so often that it is seldom either challenged or even questioned. In terms of cash output and productivity per man this statement is probably true, but one needs to look further into employment needs, ecological problems and energy usage before it is certain that one can accept it completely.

The agricultural output of the United Kingdom, of which England contributes the major part, is, at £12 billion a year, the same as the combined agricultural outputs of Australia and New Zealand and almost the same as that of Canada (Australia and New Zealand is thirty-six times larger than the United Kingdom and Canada forty-five times).

To understand why the farmers of England have intensified their farming one must look back to the early nineteenth century. When the Napoleonic wars had ended in 1815 the farmers of England were providing all the food necessary to feed the entire population of eleven million people. One-third of the working population were then engaged in farming, and ninety per cent of the land was farmed by tenant farmers. By this time the major forests had been cleared and most of the arable lands had been enclosed.

For the next fifty years English farming went through a period of almost unbridled prosperity. There was a five-fold increase in the urban population and farmers were encouraged to grow as much food as possible to feed the seventeen million people in England in 1865. During this period farmers were protected from foreign competition and although the original

Weather: The greatest influence on every farmer's activity and profit is the weather. Although England is blessed with a moderate climate there are times when extremes of climate, high or low temperatures, high rainfall or drought, can adversely affect farmers. Farmers in the eastern half of England suffered badly in the disastrously wet summer of 1987: in many areas of East Anglia grain yields were halved, quality reduced and harvesting costs trebled. Autumn cultivations were also affected so badly that there will be a deleterious effect on many farmers' 1988 harvest. Because prices paid to farmers are in some cases dependent upon government support, sometimes upon European competition and also upon world prices, there is not usually a direct co-relation between national yield and local price. Before the days of cheap and efficient transportation of food farmers tended to satisfy local demand and if there was a local shortage the price would inevitably be high. Last year's wet harvest in East Anglia was counterbalanced, as far as shortages were concerned, by a reasonable harvest in central and western England and by a bumper harvest in France.

Corn Laws were repealed in 1845 other, still stringent, import duties were applied which consolidated the farmers' strong position by effectively preventing all imports of grain below a given price.

Grain producers were guaranteed substantial profits. It was not possible to import milk, meat and butter until the introduction of refrigeration in steamships in the 1870s.

Grain prices, which had been at the record level of £28 a ton during the Napoleonic wars (not to be equalled again even in cash terms until 1973), fell only gradually during the next fifty years. In 1868 wheat was still fetching £14 a ton, which gave farmers ample profits and encouraged them to increase the acreage grown. New land was brought into cultivation and fallowing of land ceased. Additional land was reclaimed from the sea in the Wash and the fertile Fenlands were drained by pumping, thus converting grazing fields into top quality arable land.

Improvements in husbandry techniques and better tools, supplied by an expanding home agricultural machinery in-dustry, enabled yields of wheat to increase by thirty per cent, to three-quarters of a ton an acre by 1870. Increased numbers of livestock enabled greater amounts of farmyard manure to be applied to the arable land, while guano and Chilean nitrates were imported at an economic price. Superphosphates were manufactured in English factories.

A government subsidy, the first of many to follow in later years, was given to landowners and farmers to under-drain land with clay tile pipes: this improved the soil structure and enabled earlier planting, thereby lengthening the growing season. At the same time the mole plough was invented which raised crop yields.

In the middle of the nineteenth century the coming of the threshing machine, driven by steam engines, enabled farmers to abandon the flail, while the scythe took over from the sickle for cutting the corn. This period is recorded as the golden age of English farming and with good reason.

Dramatically and totally unexpectedly in the mid-1870s, depression struck English farming with a force that unsettled

Pruning Hedgerow Willows: It is almost unheard of for a farmer to lay-off his workers during the slacker months of the winter, as happens in so many other industries. Farmers use this time to catch up on general farm maintenance work, perhaps hedging and ditching or repairing buildings and machinery.

Unfortunately the specialist able to 'lay' a hedge is a rare breed of craftsman today. The modern system of machine cutting may make hedges look unsightly for a week or two but provided this work is carried out at the right time of the year by a skilled operator the cutting will encourage good bottom growth in the hedge, which is what one wants: it not only helps to make the hedge stockproof but also provides shelter and nesting sites for wildlife. With the ever increasing cost of new machinery farmers are keeping their equipment longer and are, therefore, having to pay greater attention to regular maintenance and repairs.

the countryside for many years. All the import duties on grain were repealed and cheap imports of grain flowed into England from the newly established prairies of the United States of America. Ocean shipping rates fell in line with the increasing amount to be transported and newly established railways in the USA meant that grain could reach its eastern seaboard very cheaply. At the same time the advent of refrigeration in cargo vessels meant that Australia, New Zealand and even Argentina could export meat, butter and cheese to England at competitive prices.

In the twenty years from 1891 over 180,000 farm workers (eighteen per cent of the labour force) were dismissed, and some ten per cent of farmers (25,800) left the land. The next ten years saw a further 160,000 farm workers forced to leave agricultural employment.

The slump meant that wool prices halved and the price of wheat dropped to a low of under £5 a ton in 1894, while cattle and sheep prices also dropped dramatically. The only two areas of farming that were not affected were fresh milk production and the growing horticultural sector, both groups being able to supply fresh produce to the growing urban sector.

By the start of the First World War in 1914 more than half of the food consumed in England was imported. For the five years of the war and for just two years after it English agriculture enjoyed a minor boom with, for example, wheat prices reaching £18 a ton. But this was to be short-lived and during the 1920s and the 1930s wheat prices fell until by 1934 they were down to just over £4 a ton—and once again there was a massive depression in the countryside. Good land changed hands in the 1930s for less than £3 an acre, and the farming survivors were those who abandoned intensive farming and reverted to what became known as 'dog and stick farming'—farming, that is, in the most basic way possible.

The Second World War and the resulting sea-blockade of

Oasthouses in Kent: Hop growing was at its zenith in England in 1885 with over seventy-one thousand acres of hops grown right across the kingdom. Today the main hop growing areas are Kent, Sussex, Hampshire, Hereford and Worcestershire, but only 12,500 acres are grown in all. However, our new seedless hop varieties, such as Target and Yeoman, will hopefully re-open the brewers' doors (or vats) around the world to English hops. As a result the acreage could well increase by fifty per cent over the next ten years.

There are many hop farmers who still remember the massive exodus of hop-pickers from the East End of London prior to the Second World War who looked upon hand hop-picking as a worthwhile paid holiday: generations of families would return to the same farms year after year. Today all the hops are picked by machine—efficiently, speedily and economically. With the reduction in the acreage of hops grown and the change from the traditional on-farm drying towards centralised operations many of the picturesque oasthouses have been converted into highly desirable dwellings.

England which started in 1939 meant that once again food had to be home produced (at the outbreak of war only thirty per cent of the food consumed was in this category) and farming, and farmers, returned to a period of prosperity. The forty million inhabitants of England had to be fed and the tragic losses of the North Atlantic convoys, in both men and materials, inspired farmers to produce more and more food. Land that had never seen the plough was ripped up by the all-mighty gyrotiller, powered by steam engines, and was sown with corn.

Real horse power worked alongside the new-fangled tractors and at last the £2-an-acre subsidy for ploughing-up land that had been introduced in 1936 began to be taken up. Farmers who before had only farmed with stock and grassland had to learn the complicated techniques needed for growing grain, and this they did with great success.

Young women were drafted into the Women's Land Army and the production on England's farms increased by over forty per cent during the six years of the war. By 1946 nearly half the food consumed in England was home grown. 'Food at any price' had been the wartime cry and in 1947 the Agricultural Act perpetuated this attitude, thus helping to finance a stable and prosperous home agriculture during the next twenty-five years, giving guaranteed prices that were generous by all previous standards.

Annual price reviews during this period at which the farming industry was represented by the National Farmers' Union, were held by the government of the day, and, in spite of adverse publicity from time to time, farmers' incomes were guaranteed at a level which gave them confidence to re-invest their profits in their farms.

The countryside and the farmers, in economic terms, blossomed. But critics would maintain that in some ways the countryside suffered because of this incentive for ever more food production. During the forty years between the end of the Second World War and 1985, 100,000 miles of hedgerows were removed in England to make way for larger fields to enable

Ditching: Throughout England the old-time manual ditch digger has been superseded by a tractor-mounted ditcher which is capable of clearing existing ditches and digging new ones with speed and efficiency. Clean ditches play a vital role in carrying unwanted water to carriers and to our main rivers to provide the drainage to enable the land to be farmed efficiently. Contrary to popular myth, the better drained the field the better will be its water retention capabilities in dry weather for drainage improves the soil structure and also allows plant roots to grow deeper without

becoming waterlogged.

Farmers in the 1800s understood the value of underfield draining using clay pipes and many thousands of acres were drained by French prisoners-of-war at that time. These pipes in the heavy impermeable clay soils were often sunk too deep (the value of permeable filling not being fully understood) and they tended to become sealed by the clay subsoil and thus non functioning. But many of these drainage pipes have more recently been incorporated into new schemes and are still running today.

more economic use to be made of the ever-larger machinery. Heath, moor, bog and wetlands were drained and almost a million acres of the semi-natural landscape were brought into food production.

Critics tend to overlook that during this same period there was an increase of 300,000 acres in the area of woodland in

An Apple Orchard in Herefordshire: Of the eighty-three thousand acres of orchards in England (the three main fruit-growing areas being Kent and Sussex, East Anglia, and Worcester and Hereford) thirty-six thousand are producing dessert apples and seventeen thousand cooking apples. An average apple yield is six tonnes to the acre, although cider apples (grown on ten thousand acres) will yield less than half this amount. Historically fruit farmers tended to concentrate on supplying the home market totally for very limited periods, but gradually over the past twenty years more sophisticated management has developed better handling and more controlled storage, allowing English apples to be marketed over a much longer period. Improved marketing has contributed to an increased demand for home grown apples now that the consumer is aware of the unique flavour of the English apple. Cider apple growers are usually contracted to a particular processor, who, in many cases, will also own many acres of his own fruit trees.

England, although conifers rather than hardwoods were planted: in fact, hardwood forests decreased by about twenty-five per cent, while the conifer area increased by over four hundred per cent. The majority of new woodlands were planted by the Forestry Commission or by companies acting on behalf of absentee landlords who were encouraged to plant trees by extremely generous fiscal legislation.

The reduction in hardwoods was exacerbated when, during the 1960s, Dutch elm disease took its toll in the countryside and nearly twenty million trees were destroyed. Little could be done to stop the spread of the disease but gradually the affected trees were felled and the changed vista became accepted.

During the twentieth century, fiscal legislation favouring the owner-occupier over the landlord caused the percentage of tenant farmers to fall to less than thirty per cent compared with the ninety per cent tenant occupancy at the turn of the century. Onerous taxation against landlords persuaded many to move into farming the land themselves rather than re-letting when tenancies fell vacant. This reduced opportunities for young men to enter farming as tenants but increased their chances of finding positions as professional farm managers.

Since the Second World War there has been a great desire amongst people who were not born and raised on farms to enter the farming industry. Those who had the courage and the capital have invested their time and energy, as well as their skills and their cash, in buying or tenanting land: these are the pioneers of modern farming. They have introduced new ideas which have benefitted the farming industry as a whole. Those who had the courage but not the capital trained as farm managers and they too have been responsible for many useful innovations.

Inevitably there has been a consistent over supply of these enthusiasts and many have given of their talents to the advisory and ancillary industries to everyone's benefit.

England has been fortunate, too, in the quality of her farmworkers—unmatched elsewhere. The general farmworker of fifty years ago has been replaced by highly trained and well-

Oilseed Rape: This crop spread rapidly over the face of rural England during the nineteen seventies and eighties: this year over eight hundred thousand acres of this oil producing crop were harvested, yielding over a million tonnes of oilseed. Oilseed rape blooms in May adding a brilliant yellow (and a sweet smell) to the tapestry of the countryside. Over production, and the resulting falling prices, will reduce the acreage devoted to this crop in the future. The attraction of oilseed rape to the farmer and the reason why its acreage in England has increased eighty times in the past twenty years, is because of a combination of substantial price increases (tenfold in twelve years) and because it provides an excellent break-crop for cereals. It has the added attraction of being capable of being grown and harvested using farm machinery that every cereal grower already possesses. A good winter sown crop can yield over a tonne-and-a-half to the acre, but to obtain these yields it has to be sown by early September which does create a high labour demand at an already busy time on most arable farms.

motivated stockmen and tractor drivers. The majority of workers in the farming industry today are highly skilled technicians who take a pride in their work and enjoy a job satisfaction that is rarely present in other industries.

The amount of economic output that can be achieved by one skilled man with his tractor and implement is so much greater than that achieved by a manual worker that one seldom sees a tractor driver out of his cab today: hedging, ditching, goods handling—all these and more are mechanised to ensure the best working conditions for the employee and the greatest economic return for the farmer.

Today farmers have become the victims of their own success: agriculture is still one of the nation's largest industries directly employing over six hundred thousand men and women and providing jobs for a further seven hundred thousand in directly connected ancillary industries. The outstanding productivity increases in farming have resulted in retail food prices falling

Ploughing: During the 1970s there was a movement away from ploughing the land after cereal crops had been harvested, especially if winter sown crops were to follow. However, the realisation of the long term beneficial effects of ploughing have reversed this trend and, on all but the lightest land, mouldboard ploughs are once again the first line implement for the arable farmer: the largest are capable of ploughing twenty acres a day, inverting up to twenty thousand tonnes of soil.

The major problem facing the farmer (especially those on heavier land) who try to economise by using a cultivator rather than a mouldboard plough is the smearing effect upon the soil and also the way in which cultivated stubbles fail to dry out as fast as ploughed land. In difficult autumn weather conditions farmers will only plough land that can be immediately cultivated and drilled, thus minimising the weather risk. An added attraction of a well ploughed field is that all the previously germinated weeds will be under an inverted sod and many will not therefore survive. Thus the weeds will not be able to compete with the emerging crop.

consistently in real terms and continuing to fall. Agriculture contributes £2.5 billion a year more to the nation's balance of trade than it did ten years ago. The tributes go on and on.

But sadly farmers have not heeded the warning signs and have largely ignored the changing needs of the market place. Farmers are now producing surpluses of food that are too expensive for taxpayers to continue to support. So once again in the long history of farming, price cuts and other penalties are being imposed upon those farmers who have done no more than respond successfully to the constant exhortations and financial inducements of successive governments.

Spraying in Shropshire: The sprayer is one of the most used tools on farms today. It is capable of applying to the growing crops liquid fertilisers, herbicides, fungicides, insecticides, growth regulators, haulm killers and many other liquid products used to encourage ever increasing yields. The machines are often mounted on the back of the tractor, but the larger machines, with spray booms up to eighty feet wide, are trailed behind. As the toxicity and variety of spray chemicals increase even greater care by the operators is needed. New legislation ensures that all spraying operators are fully trained, properly equipped and realise the need not only to protect themselves but to use exactly the correct quantities.

Excessive quantities would not only be a waste of money but also a danger to the crop and local wildlife and could, in extreme cases, enter underground reservoirs with serious results. Farmers fully appreciate the need for skilled handling of sprays and are dealing responsibly with this potential hazard.

Politics

IN 1973, after two abortive attempts, Britain was allowed to join an enlarged European Community, with a five-year transition period to adjust.

Free trade in agriculture gave way to almost total protectionism within the frontiers of the Community: agricultural policy in England became even more complex with its greater reliance on policy dictated by Europe. There were further complications because Britain did not join the European Monetary System; thus changes in exchange rates between Britain and other countries in the Community caused imbalance between countries in farm prices and left great scope for political manoeuvering and distortions caused by the resulting Green Currencies.

Farms in England, with an average size of 132 acres, are considerably larger than those in mainland Europe: in Greece, at the other extreme, farm size averages but ten acres—this is after excluding any holdings of less than two-and-a-half acres. In England at the present time less than 2.5 per cent of the working population are engaged in agriculture, whilst even the efficient agricultural industry of France employs seven per cent of the nation's workers on their farms: Spain, Portugal and Greece employ nearer thirty per cent.

For the first ten years following Britain's entry into the European Community, England's farmers were encouraged by a combination of exhortation and financial reward to expand their production, and this they did with commendable success. Wheat production in England has more than tripled since entry into the EEC, barley output has increased by thirty per

The Dairy Event: The Royal Association of British Dairy Farmers, established in 1876, has held 102 annual dairy shows. Here at the Stonleigh showground well over a hundred exhibitors of dairy cattle take pride in presenting their animals in pristine condition. Years of careful breeding, months of preparing the animals for the Show and hours of laundering, 'hairdressing' and pedicuring ensure that the animals are looking their best. Also at The Dairy Event there are over three hundred trade stands—unique at a specialist show.

Whereas in the past the conformation of a dairy cow was often considered to be of the greatest importance, today it is the performance of the animal that is paramount—and animals are judged accordingly. In spite of its comparatively small size the RABDF is a most enlightened and powerful lobby for the English dairy farmer.

Farmers increasingly appreciate that the best place to come to the right decisions about future equipment usage is at working demonstrations and it is at this type of show that many farmers decide what equipment to buy.

A Suffolk stream

cent and milk production has increased by fifteen per cent (with no increase in cow numbers).

Due to the European tariff barriers (often the duties imposed on imports are greater than the cost of the product) and high prices, European farmers, like the English, increased production to an extent that astounded the politicians. Self-sufficiency in almost every product was first achieved and then exceeded as production throughout Europe soared: stores bulged with the surplus. France produced twice as much wheat as she needed, Belgium two-and-a-half times the amount of sugar she required, Holland nearly five times the amount of butter she could consume and England fifty per cent more barley. The most extreme example was in oil seed rape production where high Community prices encouraged English farmers to expand their production from 10,000 tonnes in 1970 to a million tonnes in 1987.

With the exception of sheep, goat meat and venison, every major product grown in Europe is now in over-supply.

Intervention stores in Europe in 1987 were holding over a million tonnes of butter, fourteen million tonnes of cereals, 750,000 tonnes of milk powder and 700,000 tonnes of beef, plus 250,000 tonnes of olive oil. These commodities were all deteriorating and were in no way contributing to the economic welfare of farmers.

In 1987 it was estimated that the Common Agricultural Policy was costing the European taxpayer £60 million a day. Of this, two-thirds, or £40 million a day, was being spent on buying, financing, storing and ultimately disposing of the surplus products with quite a bit more lost through fraud.

But the first real indication that all was not healthy, that food production at any price was not a long-term political practicality, came in the early 1980s. Politicians still continued to clamour nationally for greater food production, but on the international scene the subsidised sales of products, surplus to the national needs, started to disrupt world food markets.

The USA and the EC were outstanding amongst the food trading countries of the world in that they were prepared to undercut their rivals at almost any cost to themselves and regardless of the effect on the stability of the world's markets.

The continuing under-performance by Russian agriculture appeared as the only bright spot for the West with its surpluses, and Russia became the dumping ground of the West's unwanted food. The cost to the taxpayers of the USA and the EC was exhorbitant. 'Produce as much food as you can' ceased to be the politicians' cry on March 31st 1984. On that day the agricultural ministers of the ten nations of the European Community (Spain and Portugal had yet to join) agreed that, as from the second day of April, milk quotas would be imposed on all milk production in the Community. English dairy farmers had to reduce production by nine per cent in the first year and in subsequent years further reductions in quota were imposed.

The lack of preparation and the inept way in which quotas were imposed reflected very badly upon the ministers and governments concerned. It threw the whole of the dairy industry into chaos. Dairy cow prices halved, farmers stopped feeding concentrated food to their cows, and young dairy stock as well as surplus cows were slaughtered, causing dramatic damage to beef producers as well when prices fell in line with the excess killings. It took two years before this damage was overcome, and there are still a great many injustices to tenant dairy farmers as to who owns the quota, the landlord or the tenant?

The advent of quotas led to the almost total demise of the English dairy equipment manufacturing industry and dairy feed compounders have also been adversely affected.

Politicians seem loath to accept the responsibilities that go with the power that they have over the destiny of farmers and subsequently over the whole countryside. For example, no thought at all appears to have been given to the dramatic effects that had to result from the imposition of milk quotas at literally forty-eight hours notice. Had more consideration been

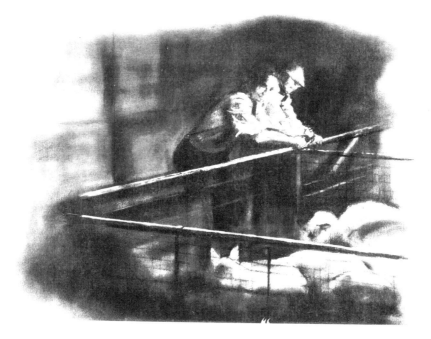

given then, whilst the cut back in milk production would have been equally, if not more, effective, the farmers and the ancillary trades would have had time to adjust to the new situation.

Perhaps one day politicians everywhere will learn that agricultural production is not like a factory conveyor belt to be slowed down or speeded up at the touch of a button. (For example from the time of the conception of a dairy calf it is nearly three years before it produces milk.) What is desperately needed in order that there should be a closer understanding between farmers, the public and the politicians is the implementation of a five year rolling strategic plan for agriculture. This plan would, with annual adjustments, give farmers sufficient warning to meet any changes necessary to provide the nation with its agricultural and environmental needs.

A Sugarbeet Factory at Bury St Edmunds: This is one of thirteen beet-processing factories in England. They handle over 8 million tonnes (from half a million acres) of beet every year, producing around one and a quarter million tonnes of pure sugar, which is enough to supply half the domestic market. The rest of the sugar needed for our home market is imported, mainly from Commonwealth cane sugar producers. The factories open at the start of beet harvesting, usually about the end of September and close at the end of January when all the beet has been processed.

Farmers are contracted to the beet processors and all the fourteen thousand growers are on a rigidly enforced quota. The price a farmer receives for his beet will obviously depend upon his yield, but deductions or additions to the price are made dependent upon the variation of its sugar content from sixteen per cent. Penalties are imposed on farmers who send in beet to the factories with a high dirt tare and so most beet is clamped on the edge of the beet field, preferably on concrete for ease of handling. It is subsequently loaded by a fore-end tractor mounted loader onto a conveyor which allows much of the dirt to fall through to the ground rather than to be loaded on to the lorries. In 1987, for the first time, an isolated case of rhysomania was found in a crop of beet: this can be a terrible problem in sugar beet and it is fervently hoped that no more will occur.

Dairying

MILK production has been, and indeed still is, the backbone of the English agricultural industry. More than half of the agricultural land in this country is devoted to feeding dairy herds and their followers, and a large minority of farmers depend upon dairying for their livelihood.

The structure of dairy farming is changing constantly. In 1960 the average size of the English dairy herd was seventeen cows. Today it is seventy.

In 1960, of the total 2.5 million cows, over seventy thousand were still being milked by hand. Thirty thousand herds then comprised less than eight cows and there were fewer than one hundred and fifty herds with more than a hundred. Today there are ten thousand herds, one-third of the total, each with more than a hundred cows: of these, half milk more than two hundred cows. The hasty imposition of milk quotas in 1984 upset the steady growth in herd size, but once it was realised that quotas were transferable, albeit with difficulty, the trend to larger herds continued, but at a slower pace. The slaughter of many dairy young-stock in the mid-1980s, as a direct result of quotas, caused a fall in numbers, and this shortage is now affecting the supply of replacements to the dairy herds.

The most dramatic change, during the past century, for the British dairy farmer was the introduction of the Friesian breed from Holland. The first importation in 1914 of just thirty-nine bulls and heifers had a great impact on English milk producers enabling them to increase their milk yields dramatically. The later importation in 1950 of ninety Dutch Friesians, at a cost of

Jersey Cows in Gloucestershire: The Jersey is a compact and good-natured animal capable of producing high quality milk. But because of the swing by dairy farmers to high yielding Friesians there are now no Jerseys kept at any of the Milk Marketing Board bull centres, although the MMB do distribute semen collected from privately owned bulls. The leading breeders of the two Channel Island breeds that are still milked in England, the Jersey and the Guernsey, have been very progressive and successful in marketing their products. Long before 'marketing' of specific products was accepted as necessary the Quality Milk Producers Association and individual CI producers were investigating ways of increasing sales. Specialised foods such as cheese, butter, yoghourts, ice cream and flavoured milk drinks were all made and sold under the Channel Island high quality label with great success.

Jerseys are, of course, particularly lovely looking beasts and the females of the species have a very placid and gentle nature which responds to the individual attention that is possible in the smaller Jersey herds. Jersey bulls however can be especially difficult to handle being of very uncertain temper.

£2500 each (equivalent to £30,000 at today's prices), had an even greater impact on English dairy herds by the use of artificial insemination.

The British Friesian and its Holstein sister account for over ninety-four per cent of dairy cows in England today. There are now only ten thousand Dairy Shorthorns, the original mainstay of dairy farmers in England. Even the top quality milk producing Jerseys, which twenty years ago numbered over one hundred thousand, now number less than thirty thousand.

The Friesian cow dominated the industry once it was appreciated that it was capable of converting grass and concentrated food extremely economically into both milk and beef. In addition, the Friesian was mainly devoid of breeding troubles, unlike so many other dairy breeds, and thus could be relied upon to produce a healthy calf each year: the male calves were retained and fattened for beef production—over fifty per cent of the beef that is produced in England is a by-product of the dairy industry.

Soon after its formation in 1933 the Milk Marketing Board, effectively a producer controlled co-operative, developed a highly efficient system of artificial insemination on a national scale, which meant that even the smallest herd could benefit by using high quality bulls which had been selected and tested by the Board. Private breeders were responsible for breeding the bulls and the cows necessary to enable the Board to carry out its development programme and the contribution of these private breeders to the success of the dairy industry must not be underestimated.

Nearly a million inseminations are now carried out on English dairy farms each year and over eighty per cent of cows inseminated are successfully impregnated by the first service. It is because of the success of artificial breeding that only twelve per cent of dairy herds rely solely on natural mating—although the majority of the herds that do rely on artificial insemination also

Friesian Cows: The average size of dairy herds in England is sixty cows: this is, of course, much larger than the average size of herds on the mainland of Europe where in most countries the average is less than half this number. Italy still has less than ten cows in its average herd. The black and white cow, be it the Friesian in England, the Schwazbunt in Germany or the Zwartbunt in Holland, predominates in almost every European country.

In England even twenty years ago other breeds still accounted for thirty per cent of the national herd. Ayrshires then numbered over a quarter of a million, today there are fewer than fifty thousand: Channel Islanders were over two hundred and fifty thousand strong, now there are fewer than a third this number: breeds, such as the Dairy Shorthorn, the Red Poll and the South Devon together now number fewer than sixteen thousand cows and their numbers are still declining. The counties of Cumbria, Cheshire and Somerset are the ones with the largest number of dairy cows, each with around one hundred and fifty thousand cows. Cheshire, however, has the highest stocking density with a cow for every four acres in the county. One wonders what the stocking rate is for the two thousand five hundred dairy cows that are still milked in Greater London?

have a bull to run with the heifers for ease of management.

Improvements in breeding and feeding resulted, until quota imposition, in large annual increases in yields from individual cows until in 1983 the average yield peaked at 1118 gallons, up by fifty per cent from 700 gallons just twenty-five years earlier.

Quota imposition in 1984, which caused an immediate cut-back in production of nine per cent, was so unexpected and so badly thought out that the immediate result was complete chaos and confusion. Over-reaction by farmers resulted in the slaughter of excessive numbers of cows and an even greater reduction in the number of dairy heifers bred and retained. Farmers also cut out concentrate feeding to such an extent that, combined with the reduction in cow numbers, milk production fell by over two hundred and twenty million gallons in just one year.

Milk quotas were imposed right across the broadest spectrum of dairy farmers. The cut in output was the same nine per cent whether the farmer milked twenty cows or two hundred.

Since it was the smaller dairy farmers that suffered the most, it was those areas peculiar to small-scale dairy farming that were in the worst economic plight. Counties such as Cornwall, Devon, Somerset and Lancashire were particularly badly affected, and many of the smaller dairy farmers could not survive on the reduced output that they were allowed to produce. Amongst the most unfortunate were those dairy farmers who were in the process of expanding their herds and who had in many cases put up new buildings to accommodate the intended increase but who were unable to obtain a quota other than that based upon their original herd size in 1983. The margin that they could obtain from this minimal quota would certainly not be enough to service the interest charges that they would have incurred on the money invested not only in the additional housing but in many cases the extra cows would already have been purchased. Many small dairy farmers in this predicament had no alternative but to give up farming altogether.

Equally badly hit were tenant farmers who suffered from the

Milking Time: The Fresian is the most prolific of all the dairy breeds. Together with its close relative, the Holstein, they now account for over ninety four per cent of dairy cows in England today. The Milk Marketing Board maintains a stud of over six hundred Friesian/Holstein bulls and inseminates nearly a million cows a year. This predominance will increase as the science of transplanting of embryos increases. Already it is possible for commercial cows to be implanted with the embryos taken from high quality animals thus enabling a rapid build up of quality breeding. The original high cost of the operation has been decreasing rapidly as techniques are perfected and as demand increases. Selective breeding by this method is now a practical commercial proposition and it is gratifying to think that English pioneers in this field have led the world. Deep frozen bull semen has been exported for many years, but now the deep frozen embryo is earning this country considerable profits as well as much praise.

The new 'multiple ovulation embryo transfer' system has the potential to double the rate of genetic progress compared with the current bull progeny testing methods.

legislation imposed which implied that quotas belonged not to the dairy farmers but to the land. Thus for two and a half years, from quota imposition on April 2nd 1984 until September 1986, when the law changed, one thousand tenants who gave up dairy farming, or transferred their businesses to other farms, received no compensation whatsoever for their quotas from their landlords.

The Agricultural Act of 1986 went a little way along the road to compensating tenant farmers for quota value, but the bitterness resulting from the unfair treatment by some landlords (acting within the unfair law) still rankles and it will be many years before the damage caused to the landlord/tenant relationship will be healed.

The impact of milk quotas has had such a dramatic effect on the economics of dairy farming that the quota is now worth much more than the cows and sometimes even more than the land itself. For example, in 1988, a good Friesian dairy cow was worth £550, an acre and a quarter of land upon which to keep the cow was worth £1250, while a five-thousand litre quota (1100 gallons) was worth £1500.

There are some who decry the transferability of quotas, suggesting that it is in some way unfair, or, more correctly, that quotas have bestowed a windfall upon the milk producer. However, were milk quotas to be rigidly fixed to the farm upon which they were imposed, it would lead to total stagnation, gross inefficiency and ultimate bankruptcy of large sectors of the industry. Transferability of sugarbeet and potato quotas has led to increased efficiency amongst these growers and should be used as an example for milk producers to follow.

Technical, genetic management and other improvements in farming led to constant productivity improvements and there has been but little objection to these natural and progressive

Silage Making: The advent of the forage harvester in the late 1950s revolutionised silage making. The forage harvester enabled grass to be either cut, or picked up if pre-cut and wilted, and blown directly into a trailer, either hitched behind the forage harvester or running alongside. The speed, efficiency and reliability of these machines enabled farmers to make large quantities of good quality silage very economically (a dairy cow can consume up to eight tonnes during the winter). As a result the majority of farmers gave up the hazards of haymaking in the difficult English climate as a means of conserving their grass for winter consumption.

The problem which then occurred for silage makers was how to manage the effluent, especially in a wet season. In a dry period there should be no effluent at all from well-made wilted silage with a dry matter of more than thirty per cent. But early cut, immature, but potentially high quality, silage may well have less than seventeen per cent dry matter—and unless efficient wilting can be achieved effluent discharge is a problem, just as it is for all silage in wet weather. The effluent is highly damaging if allowed to enter water courses and so most farmers now have a catchment pit to collect the effluent; every one per cent of excess moisture can produce two gallons of effluent for every tonne ensiled. Effluent when fresh can be a valuable feed additive but the quantities and timing usually mean that it has to be wasted by being spread on to conveniently placed fields when conditions allow.

steps. But the reaction by a few milk producers to the first real progress in biotechnology, or genetic engineering, has been to remind one of the Luddites, or even the notorious Swing riots that hit rural communities in the 1830s. Then it was the advent of the threshing machine that provoked the anger: today it is Bovine Somatotrophin.

BST are the accepted initials for a product that it is difficult to understand and even more difficult to pronounce. Bovine Somatotrophin is probably going to be one of the greatest technological benefits to milk production that we have seen in our lifetime. BST is a naturally occuring hormone in the dairy cow that can be artificially increased by injection to enable either the same amount of milk to be produced when feeding significantly less food or more milk to be produced with the same amount of food.

This is a valuable step forward that could be thwarted even before the trials are complete by ill-informed criticism. The problem that should be exercising the minds of both the critics and the supporters of BST should be how best to utilise the twenty per cent of the land that will be released from providing feed for the cows.

The precarious financial position of many dairy farmers could be mitigated greatly by increasing the efficiency of their operations and the use of BST could be one very important step in this direction.

The British consumer is unique in the world in being able to have fresh milk delivered to the doorstep. Every day nearly twenty million pint milk bottles are delivered to fourteen million households by forty-eight thousand dairy roundsmen in England. In other countries, when doorstep deliveries ceased and milk had to be collected from the shop, there was a significant reduction in milk consumption, up to forty per cent in some countries.

The production, processing, transport and delivery of milk in England is a triumph of coordination and skill which could well be used as a model for other commodities.

Farm buildings in Surrey: Today's farm buildings are designed with technical and practical considerations taking precedence over aesthetics. This was not always the case. In the picture what appears to be a Gothic tithe barn is, in fact, an early Victorian copy and is used today to store fertilizer. The stew pond in the foreground, originally dug to produce carp for the Cistercian monks of the local abbey, in now stocked with trout and is used by local fishermen wishing to improve their casting skills. This provides a useful ancillary income for the farmer-owner.

Sheep

MANY of the lovely buildings in our small country towns, and indeed many of the towns themselves, are there because of the prosperity of wool merchants in mediaeval times. In the early years sheep were kept primarily for their wool, but today their meat is the main product, with wool but a small bonus.

There have been, and still are, an excessive number of breeds of sheep and cross-breds. There has been little rationalisation in the selection of breeds and the sheep farmer can make his choice from nearly fifty accredited pure-breeds and even more recognised half-breeds.

The inate conservatism of the traditional sheep farmer has

inhibited the widespread acceptance of the new sheep breeds, such as the Colbred, the Meatlinc, the Oldenberg and the Texel. This is in marked contrast to the dairy industry where most of the traditional breeds have given way to the Friesians and Holsteins, and even the beef farmers have accepted the new continental breeds to their undoubted financial gain.

Today there are over eight million ewes and some two hundred thousand rams in England on forty-nine thousand farms, the majority of which are kept for producing meat as a main product. The total amount of sheepmeat produced in England every year exceeds one hundred and fifty thousand tonnes. In addition over twenty-one thousand tonnes of wool

Sheep Shearing in Shropshire: A ewe has to be sheared once a year and a good sheep shearer is able to shear thirty ewes an hour. A favoured modern technique is to shear the in-lamb ewes prior to housing them for lambing: this allows the ewe to be comfortable even with dense stocking. Different breeds of sheep will yield a wide variety of both quality and quantity of wool. For example, a Suffolk ewe could yield up to eight pounds of upper medium quality fleece, while a Welsh Mountain might produce only three pounds of very poor quality wool. There are no British breeds of sheep in the Australian Merino class for producing top quality wools.

Wool marketing is one of the success stories of the English farming scene and the establishment of the British Wool Marketing Board in 1950

relieved sheep farmers of the problem of handling their wool marketing and gave them great benefits of scale. England's forty-nine thousand sheep farmers produced over twenty-one thousand tonnes of wool worth over £22m (or nearly £3 for every ewe) in 1987. Producers are paid for their wool according to the weight, the type, the grade and the cleanliness. Everyone with more than four sheep has to be registered and their wool clip must be marketed through the Wool Board, except for small amounts sold directly by producers to hand-weavers.

The Wool Board exports over two-thirds of its wool to thirty-six countries with Belgium, China, Japan and France topping the list and buying half the total exported.

are produced every year and this is increasing by six per cent a year as sheep numbers increase. Although there was an importation of the Fries Malkschaap, from Holland and Germany, a breed of sheep for milking, there has been no significant growth in the production of sheep milk.

A good British Friesland milking ewe can yield a hundred and twenty-five gallons of milk in an eight month lactation, which can be turned into sixty pounds of top quality soft cheese. There is, in addition, the value of the fleece and the meat. In view of the prolificacy of this breed and the increasing demand for ewe cheese, against the oversupply of cows' milk, one would expect some growth in milk production from sheep.

The choice the farmer has to make when selecting the most economic breed of sheep for his own requirements will depend upon his location and the topography of his farm. The hill and upland breeds, such as the Welsh, the Swaledales and the Cheviots, are capable of surviving the rigours of the harsh winters and high rainfall to be found on the moors and in the uplands of the south-west and the north of England. Few, if any, of the lambs born in these areas grow to slaughter weight in their first summer, so they are sold as 'store' lambs after weaning, to be fattened in lowland areas where the climate, and therefore the food availability, is kinder. The upland ewes themselves, as they become older and less able to withstand the harsh conditions, are sold to lowland farms where they will continue to breed economically for a few more years. The lowland farmer will usually cross these upland ewes with a longwool breed, such as a Border Leicester, to produce cross-bred ewes which form the major portion of the sheep breeds kept on the lowland farms. Later these cross-bred offspring, hardy and with good milking and mothering ability, will themselves be mated with a downland ram, such as a Suffolk, to produce a high quality carcass for slaughter.

Gradually, as fashions and economic necessities change, more lowland arable farmers are becoming large scale sheep producers. These farmers, with the benefit of good quality land and clement weather, are able to stock their ewes at up to ten to the acre, while the upland farmer will seldom achieve even one ewe to every acre. Likewise, while the lowland sheep farmer will hope for a lambing percentage of nearly two hundred per cent, the hill farmer will expect, in a good season, but eighty per cent.

Suffolk Half-breds in the Cotswolds: More and more farmers are realising that the value of their flocks is increasing to such an extent that the cost of housing the sheep (even at the current building cost of £100 a ewe) is becoming justified, especially in areas like the Cotswolds where sudden heavy winter snowfalls are a real hazard. When sheep and beef prices were comparatively low compared with the prices received for grain in the nineteen sixties and seventies many Cotswold farmers ploughed their grassland and grew very mediocre crops of corn. Now that this price relationship is altering, farmers are resurrecting their old shepherding skills and restocking with sheep. Fences, walls and hedges which were allowed to deteriorate during the corn growing period are now being re-established and the whole appearance of the Cotswolds is changing for the better.

Yorkshire Dales

Thus the economic pressures on the hill and marginal land farmers are increasing. It is essential that if the nation wants to preserve its beautiful uplands and moors—in the Lake District, the Dales and similar—then these farmers have to be rewarded for their role as custodians of the land.

Perhaps the major improvement in sheep husbandry that has recently taken place is the continuing move to house the ewe flock before they lamb down in the spring. The diehards still believe that it is the shepherd who gains most from this as he then avoids the worst of the hard winter nights, but more flock owners now accept that not only will the ewes, with of course their lambs, improve in condition when housed, with

Lambing: Lambing in a purpose-built barn is not only better for the sheep but also for the shepherd. The sheep benefit from the shelter of the building and there is less likelihood of the lambs being separated from their dams after birth, and the shepherd is better able to tend his flock in more kindly conditions and in a more confined space. In the more clement climatic areas sheep farmers lamb their flocks earlier than in the harsher areas so that the resulting fat lambs can catch the higher priced Easter market. This means that the ewes must be mated in July or August to lamb down in December or January.

Most breeds and crossbreeds start their natural breeding season in late August so hormone treatment is often used to bring the ewes into season earlier. Lowland flocks aim to average two lambs per ewe and to achieve this requires skilful management. The upland and marginal land sheepmen will lamb their flocks much later, in late April and early May, to coincide with the start of their much later grass growth. Few of these ewes will produce twins and the upland flock will seldom exceed one lamb sold per ewe.

consequent reduction in losses, but the pastures also will benefit from being rested for a while from the sheep.

Although the prosperity of England depended upon the production of wool until the onset of the industrial revolution in the 1750s, and although there was a sharp decline in sheep numbers in the first half of this century, England today ranks fourth in the world (after New Zealand, Scotland and Wales) for the greatest number of sheep in relation to its land area.

The gross output from the forty-seven thousand sheep farms in England now amounts to over £300 million every year from the sales of meat and wool, but with less than seven per cent of this amount coming from wool.

Suffolk Rams: Suffolk sheep, although one of the minority breeds, are kept for crossing with other breeds to improve both fecundity and wool quality. A pure bred Suffolk has the highest wool quality of all the British breeds and also produces the heaviest weight of fleece, up to about eight pounds. The popularity of both the pure-bred Suffolk and the Suffolk Cross sheep is such that, whilst still not in the top five most popular breeds, they are showing marked increases in numbers.

In the past ten years sheep in England have shown a forty-three per cent growth in numbers, and are increasing by six per cent a year. Twenty years ago England was only forty per cent self-sufficient in mutton and lamb supplies, but by 1978 this figure had risen to sixty per cent and today it is at ninety per cent and still improving. Sheepmeat exports are also increasing (by twenty per cent last year) and provide a useful contribution to Britain's balance of trade.

Beef

PRIOR to the Second World War more than half the beef consumed in England came from overseas, mainly from the ranches of North and South America. Today more than ninety-three per cent is home produced.

Although there has been a decline in the consumption of beef during this period, from an annual figure of 55 lbs down to a current 40 lbs per head, the major reasons for the greater proportion of home-produced beef on the market are two-fold. First, the growth in the number of beef cows, now 500,000, reared in England, and, secondly and more significantly, the increase in the amount of beef produced as a by-product of the dairy industry. This is a result of the dual-purpose ability of the ubiquitous Friesian dairy cow and the greater use of beef bulls on dairy cows.

Pure-bred beef cows produce enough offspring for only a small proportion of the English beef market (less than twenty per cent) but pure-bred beef bulls make a significant impact since they are largely used for crossing with dairy cows to produce calves suitable for beef. In fact this country was for many years considered to be the 'stud farm of the world'. The Aberdeen Angus and Hereford breeds especially have had a significant impact on cattle breeding throughout the world over the past century.

South American cattle grazing their coarse pampas grass tended to become heavy and unmanageable and for over a hundred years the smaller, neater bulls from this country were in great demand. Beef breeders here have tended, over the past forty years, to concentrate upon supplying this specialised market and have sometimes neglected to consider the needs of the English dairy herds with regard to beef bulls. Many of the

A Beef Yard near Bath: Almost a quarter of all the 155,000 farms in England have some form of beef enterprise, but the average number of cattle on each is only sixteen animals. On the majority of these holdings the animals are kept in old buildings that have been converted from their original use. The cost of labour, feed and bedding in these buildings is much higher than in modern purpose-built beef buildings. The cost of new farm buildings is now extremely high in relation to product prices received by the farmer, since beef farmers' incomes have fallen significantly in real terms. A new purpose-built beef house will cost between £300 and £400 per head housed depending upon the site and method of construction. If one has to justify the expenditure and service the capital invested then this puts an added annual cost of about £60 for every animal housed: this is a formidable cost which has to be balanced by increased efficiency. As a result it is unusual to find any new beef buildings, or indeed any new farm building other than for sheep, being built during the current agricultural economic crisis.

Welsh Black

Angus and Hereford bulls became so grotesquely dwarfed that they were almost unable to perform the vital function for which they were bred. Other aesthetic considerations also took precedence (such as colour marking) over the modern needs for scientific breeding and producing off-spring that are economically acceptable to both the producer and the butcher—and ultimately to the consumer.

As a result of this failure by pedigree beef breeders to face the changing requirements of the marketplace, importations of foreign beef bulls began to take place. At the same time some countries, notably America, Canada and Argentina, bred their own pedigree bulls from basic British stock, and now it is these overseas Angus and Hereford herds that are supplying the world's needs for stock bulls.

The exotics, the imported bulls from the Charolais, Limousin and Simmental breeds, now play a significant role in crossing with the dairy herds of this country. Just under half of all dairy cow inseminations in England are from beef bulls, with the exotic breeds predominating. Of the one million inseminations carried out annually by the Milk Marketing Board with beef bull semen forty per cent are from the Limousin breed, with the Hereford and Charolais breeds each providing twenty per cent. The once influential Angus breed now only provides some sixty thousand inseminations a year, even less than the Simmental and the Belgian Blue separately. In all, the MMB provides semen from twenty-five different beef breeds, but

Lincoln Red cattle near The Wash: There are many thousands of acres of marshland around the Wash which provide valuable grazing during the dryer summer months. The Lincoln Red used to be the predominant breed of cattle kept in this area, but most farmers have changed to more exotic breeds to be used both as pure breds and for crossing with other British breeds of cattle.

Like so many beef breeds the Lincoln Red is no longer a commercial proposition and is now kept solely on account of the whim and preference of the owner. Just ten years ago the Hereford breed inseminations outnumbered the Charolais three to one and the Limousin was responsible for fewer than one per cent of all inseminations. Today it is the Limousin bulls (used for thirty-seven per cent of all beef inseminations) and the Charolais (with nearly twenty per cent), which are the most popular breeds for crossing with dairy cows to produce beef calves. The Hereford is still just holding its own with the Charolais but the demand for the other traditional British breeds is insignificant.

apart from the Limousin, Hereford, Charolais, Simmental, Belgian Blue and Angus, none are significant in national terms.

In the 1960s when these bulls were first imported into England, many dairy cows, and more especially heifers, experienced very difficult calvings, but now the more scientific breeding and selection of bulls has largely solved this problem. Calves resulting from this cross-breeding have a greater genetic potential than those of pure-bred stock for quicker liveweight gain, and can produce a more acceptable carcass for the butcher.

The traditional herds of single-suckled beef cows, usually found in the hill or more marginal lands, find it difficult to compete economically with the more intensively reared cross-bred animals to be found on lowland farms, usually kept as part of a mixed farming system. Hill cow herds are mainly kept to provide suckler calves for ultimate fattening in the lowlands.

Beef breeding and beef animal management have not made

Beef Cattle in Oxfordshire: The picture shows a mixed bunch of steers being fattened for beef on the rolling slopes of Oxfordshire. The lower land, sown into cereals and rape, is Grade 3 land, while the grassland is Grade 4 and not suitable for ploughing.

As economic forces weigh ever more heavily upon the beef farmer he is intensifying his methods of production. The dairy farmer, when grazing his animals, will ensure constant rotation, and then manuring, of his pastures to make sure that he obtains maximum economic production from the grazing. The beef man, in general, has not yet followed this intensive grazing system. But in order to get the best possible returns from his grassland the progressive beef farmer is now handling his grazing regime more carefully so as to produce a larger amount of beef from every acre. Winter housing is now usual and silage the most popular forage food fed: today grass will provide eighty-five per cent of the energy requirements of beef cattle and even a hundred per cent of their protein requirements for most of their lifetime.

comparable advances to those made in the dairy industry. A number of farmers have intensified their beef system: they use cross-bred animals, house them in purpose-built buildings with controlled feeding and their pastures are heavily stocked, well fertilized and managed. But efficient beef farmers of this sort are still very much in a minority.

Single Sucklers: The traditional single suckler beef herd on our uplands calves down in the spring and after the calf (and ideally the hill farmer does not want twins) has run with its dam through the summer it is usually sold to a lowland beef fattener in the autumn. Almost half the beef produced in England today originates from the single suckler herd.

Single suckler beef systems produce calves that are ready for market at lighter weights than those calves bred out of dairy cows. This is as a result of the inherent beefing qualities and the more rapid growth rates in suckler herds. Concentrate feed usage is lower but is essential if the finished

Because of increased efficiency and financial pressures the age at which beef cattle are being slaughtered is gradually reducing: thirty years ago much of the beef would be nearly three years old at slaughter, but today the majority of stock will be ready for the butcher at under eighteen months.

The gradual replacement of the individual butcher's shop by

animal is to be ready for market at fifteen months or less. Most of the costs associated with beef production can be attributed to the cost of, and the keeping of, the cow. Thus it is vitally important that each cow calves down every twelve months with no loss of time between calving and conception and with minimum mortality of cow or calf. Stocking rate is important and with spring calving herds a cow and a calf should be kept on an acre of reasonable grassland for the best economic results: with autumn calving about one-and-a-quarter acres is the aim.

the massive supermarket chainstore is also having an effect upon the cuts of beef that are in demand, and slowly, too slowly, the breeding and management of beef animals is changing to meet this new requirement. The supermarket's main requirement is for a standardised, pre-packed, lean and mainly small cut, which needs a different type of carcass to that formerly required. Consumer taste is changing and red meat is declining in popularity: many people are eating poultry and fish rather than red meat.

The trend towards total or partial vegetarianism is growing, especially amongst the young, and the beef industry, from the producer, the processor and wholesaler to the retailer, is

putting great effort into popularising their products once more. Perhaps they should be aiming at matching American consumption of beef, which is 77 lbs for every USA citizen each year, against the English consumption of 48 lbs, and the French of over 70 lbs per person per year.

Gradually beef producers are accepting the changing needs of the marketplace; more contract arrangements are being made between breeders and producers and between producers and supermarkets, and a sense of economic realism is entering into a system of farming that has always suffered from non-progressive thought, which has led to low profit margins.

Lincoln Reds on the Fosse Way: This is not a common sight in any part of England as Lincoln Reds are a disappearing breed. The Fosse Way, built by the Roman invaders in the year AD 50, runs from Leicester to Stow on the Wold, sixty miles and predictably straight: when the Roman invaders left, the Fosse Way became one of the main sheep droveways. Today the route has the distinction of being one of the main road arteries bringing many of the quarter of a million farmers visitors to the annual Royal

Agricultural Show at Stonleigh—the highlight of the agricultural social calender. Since 1963, when the Show ceased its peripatetic existence and settled down to a permanent site, it has developed into a permanent exhibition of all aspects of rural life. The Show is the flagship of the Royal Agricultural Society of England, which has been in existence for one hundred and fifty years.

Pigs & Poultry

CENTURIES ago the English pig was a razor-backed animal wandering or herded in the forests and living off vegetable matter found beneath the trees. In the middle of the nineteenth century new strains of pigs were imported from China, which altered the whole pattern of pig farming.

From these early importations were bred the Gloucester Old Spot, the Middle White, the Berkshire, the Wessex Saddleback, and, most famous of all, the Large White. The Large White, the main breed to be used for the production of bacon, was unchallenged until the importation of the Swedish Landrace in the 1950s.

Mainly as a result of this importation, pig breeding and pig management in England have shown great progress over the last thirty years: in fact, with the possible exception of the

poultry industry, pig farming, of all aspects of farming, has shown the most dramatic improvement. What used to be an individual based enterprise, where the large majority of pig-meat consumed came from cottagers and smallholders and the pigs kept for converting the swill from the towns, has now grown into a large-scale, highly technical operation.

Gradually this century some pig farmers have increased their pig numbers but even in the 1950s, on the 60,000 pig farms in England, the average herd comprised but seven sows with a total number of pigs per farm of only forty. The national pig population was less than two-and-a-half million. Pig feed was at that time strictly controlled and it was not until 1954, when meat rationing ended in England, that pig feed became more freely available.

Today there are nearly three-quarters of a million breeding

A Hen House: The picture shows an intensive deep-litter unit capable of producing eggs cleanly and efficiently. Well-bred chickens in a well managed house will lay 280 eggs in a fifty-two-week laying period: the average price a farmer will be paid is less than 4p per egg. It is important that the atmosphere in the hen house is kept both dry and at a constant temperature if the best results are to be achieved. Egg production expanded in England rapidly during the 1970s with large-scale battery egg systems

effectively quadrupling the annual output. Since 1980 there has been a gradual decline but by 1986 it had stabilised and today there are some thirty-eight million laying birds which enable England to be ninety-nine per cent self-sufficient in eggs. The deficit is made up by imports from the European Community but price increases to the producers will mean that the home industry will expand in 1988/9 to satisfy the entire home market requirement.

pigs kept on eleven thousand farms, an average of sixty-eight sows per farm. In addition there are six million fattening pigs on fifteen thousand farms (some of which are also breeding farms) each producing an average of four hundred fattening pigs on a continuing cyclical basis with fattening being an all-year-round operation.

With the success of the new pig breeders, the number of pigs produced grew rapidly in the late 1950s and early 60s. Since then the number of pigs in England has fluctuated only slightly, mainly due to competition from imported bacon, especially from Denmark.

The English pig farmer used to have three choices open to him: he could produce a carcass suitable for pork, a carcass suitable for bacon or he could produce heavy hogs to supply the manufacturers of sausages and pies. Pigs bred and fattened for pork are slaughtered at twenty weeks, weighing 160 pounds, and those for bacon at twenty-four weeks, weighing 200 pounds. Nowadays all pigmeat markets are tending to be supplied from a pig weighing around 200 pounds: some parts of the pig are cured for bacon, others for fresh pork and the rest goes for manufacturing pies, sausages, etc.

The management factor which has the most impact on pig fattening profitability is the conversion rate of turning the food fed to the pigs into meat. With breeding it is the number of piglets weaned per sow per year that has the most effect on profitability. Financially it is the ratio of the end price to the feed price that is the determinant of profitability.

The top producers of weaner pigs at eight weeks old for subsequent fattening are achieving conversion ratios for their feed of one pound of meat produced for every one-and-a-half pounds of highly concentrated expensive feed. And these top ten per cent of pig farmers are achieving an output of over twenty-four piglets reared per sow per year. Ten years ago the comparable figure for the best pig farmers was a conversion rate of three pounds of feed for every pound of meat and an average of only twenty-one piglets reared.

Virtually all fattening animals are kept in purpose-built housing to ensure better management and also to provide ideal

Turkeys near Cambridge: This breed of turkey, uninspiringly named Big Five, has been specially bred to produce offspring that are capable of being fattened to the best possible weight in the shortest possible time. A bird of this breed can grow to 30 lbs in five months. One stag turkey is needed for every twenty hens, but breeding today is mainly by artificial insemination.

Turkey production is now an industrialised operation with great emphasis upon employing the latest techniques in feeding, housing and management.

The marketing of turkeys is a highly organised and professional example for producers of other products to follow. Indeed 'it's boo-ti-full', in broad Norfolk dialect, has now become part of the English language. Great emphasis is placed by turkey processors upon developing new products by careful selection, cutting and packaging. Turkey production is increasing and steadily encroaching upon the meat market at the expense of beef and lamb.

conditions for maximum economic gain in liveweight from the feed.

Until recently consumer preference has been for lean meat and so farmers sought to produce this at the lowest cost possible. Now there is a growing demand for what the consumer sees as naturally produced meat. As a result of this change in demand the forward-looking pig producers are concentrating on production techniques to reduce the use of preventative medicines in diets. This means less intensive methods with even a reversion to straw-based systems of housing. This change in management and feeding may show that in trying to satisfy the customer's demand for lean meat much was lost in flavour and texture in the final product.

The majority of breeding pigs are also housed, but there is a growing popularity in the keeping of sows and their litters outside. These pigs are provided with pig arks and have freedom to graze. The problems of disease, especially E. Coli, are reduced, and, given suitable free-draining land and good management, this system provides a viable economic alternative. Some five or six sows with their litters can be run on every acre and their presence provides a build-up in fertility which can be taken up by the following cereal crop when the pigs are moved

Outdoor Pig Arks: There is a great deal of interest, and also expansion, in the outdoor farrowing and raising of weaner pigs. The advantages are the considerable saving in the cost of housing and also fewer problems with disease when compared with pigs kept indoors. The ability to move the arks from field to field leaving behind extra fertility also adds to the attraction of the system. The land used for this purpose needs to be in an area with a mild, relatively dry, climate and to have good drainage.

The competitive nature of pigmeat production is such that new techniques require constantly changing housing. Today it will cost well over one thousand pounds per sow-and-litter-place to build and furnish a farrowing house and up to £100 per baconer-place for a fattening house. When one adds to this all the other needs, such as weaner-places, boar and dry sow housing, one is looking at a figure of over £1300 per sow for indoor breeding facilities and for rearing the progeny to bacon weight. This is one of the reasons why outdoor rearing and breeding of weaners is a rapidly expanding alternative since the overall cost of the outdoor housing is so much lower for rearing weaners to eight weeks old.

to fresh pastures.

Many new entrants to farming are finding that outdoor pig breeding provides a financially viable and practical way of entering farming. They rent suitable land on an annual basis from farmers happy to gain from the resulting fertility and only need the capital to purchase the breeding stock and the pig arks.

One of the growing problems facing intensive pig keepers, especially where their housing is designed to handle the manure as liquid slurry, is the disposal of the effluent. Where large-scale operations are situated on large farms the problem is not so acute for it is usually possible for the farmer to spread the slurry over adjoining fields. But it is the intensive units, with little land adjoining, which have the problems.

Perhaps this problem will hasten the move away from slurry manure systems to straw-based housing units, or even to more outdoor breeding?

The dramatic growth that has taken place in the poultry industry, in both egg and poultry meat production, is the largest in any sector of English agriculture.

Prior to the Second World War the total production of poultry meat in the whole of the United Kingdom was less than ninety thousand tonnes. Today the comparable figure is over a million tonnes. In England alone at any one time there are now fifty million chickens being fattened for meat production. Annually some 550 million birds produce 750,000 tonnes of chicken meat in England.

The poultry farm of times past has been replaced by mammoth operations using the most modern systems of management, housing, slaughter, packaging and marketing. The price of poultry meat has fallen rapidly because of these sophisticated and large-scale techniques and has resulted in chicken and turkey becoming the cheapest meat available today to the consumer, rather than being a rare family treat. Poultry meat demand has therefore shown a consistent increase at the expense of red meats, the consumption of which has gradually fallen over the past twenty years.

Ducks, geese and guineafowl contribute to poultry meat production, there being nearly two million of these birds kept for meat production.

In all, there are over three fowls of assorted species for every man, woman and child in England. It is, however, the turkey which has shown the greatest growth in production, even greater than that of the chicken. In the past thirty years the number of home-grown turkeys consumed annually has grown from one million birds to over thirty-two million birds today. The total yearly tonnage consumed now exceeds 200,000 tonnes, of which more than half is predictably eaten at Christmas. Two-thirds of the total amount of turkey meat produced in England is supplied by just two firms and there are less than two hundred producers of significance in the whole of England.

Egg production techniques have changed as dramatically as has poultry meat production, especially with the advent of battery housing for chickens. In England today, of the thirty million hens kept for egg production, over ninety per cent are kept in battery cages. These hens produce more than 6000 million eggs a year.

Although there is a great deal of vocal antipathy towards this system of egg production, the harsh world of economics decrees that the large majority of consumers will not let their hearts rule their pockets. Less than five per cent of all eggs consumed are produced by free range hens. Although the demand for free range eggs is increasing slowly their extra fifty per cent cost ensures that the battery egg will remain the market leader for many years to come.

Arable

I N the eighty years prior to the ultimate acceptance of the combine harvester, including during the Second World War, all grain was cut by a binder. This machine, originally horse-drawn and then pulled by a tractor, cut the grain about two weeks before it was ripe to avoid shedding the grains. The sheaves produced by the binder were then stooked by hand and allowed to ripen in the fields. The sheaves would then be loaded onto a trailer and carted to the cornyard where they would be stacked for subsequent threshing. All this was very labour intensive and, if it was wet after cutting and before carting, grain losses from the ripening ears could be heavy.

The one advantage this method had over cutting by a combine harvester (which cuts and threshes on the move) was that any wild oats in the crop would be cut by the binder before they ripened and fell to the ground, thus avoiding contaminating the following crop. The advent of the combine harvester caused an explosion in the wild oat population and until effective chemical sprays were developed in the 1960s wild oats were one of the major problems of the cereal farmer.

The easier, more efficient and earlier clearance of the grain crops by combine enabled post harvest cultivations to be carried out earlier: at the same time scientists were producing heavier yielding winter wheat varieties and so there was a swing to earlier sown winter wheat. On the heavier clay lands most farmers like to finish their sowing by the end of October.

Traditionally grain stubbles had been left for the convenience of the local hunt and to encourage pheasants and partridges until the land had to be prepared for spring-sown grain. With growing mechanisation and the swing to winter sowing this

Vining Peas near Boston, Lincolnshire: The area of vining peas grown in England, almost entirely for freezing, has stabilised at ninety thousand acres. Vining peas provide a very good cereal break-crop and will yield two tonnes to the acre on good land. Since vining machinery is so expensive (a self-propelled viner costs £150,000) many of the growers rely on contractors for their harvesting, which will cost around £50 a tonne (or £100 an acre). All the peas are grown on contract to the processors and have to be delivered to the freezing plants within two hours of harvesting to ensure the maximum sugar content. The planting of peas is carried out on a regular planned schedule allowing for different harvesting times based on 'heat-unit' calculations. When the crop is harvested (usually in June) the whole operation is a continuous twenty-four hour cycle with peas being picked according to the tenderometer reading, which, as its name suggests, accurately gauges the tenderness of the peas: the viners, the transport lorries and the factory are all in radio contact and this is the nearest procedure in farming to a military operation.

became impracticable and as a result the number of wild game birds fell over the years.

The heavy capital investment and the reliability of the new machinery meant that farm workers used them to their maximum and, as a result, worked long hours whenever the weather permitted. There were a few farmers who frowned upon Sunday working, but as pressures grew even these few gave way.

Encouraged by the government, farmers continued to grow more corn after the Second World War and there has been steady growth since then in arable farming. Half the total agricultural area of England is now used for arable cropping. Prior to the war less than one-third of the thirteen million tonnes of grain consumed in England was grown here.

Parity between imported and home-grown cereals was achieved by the end of the war and home production went on increasing while imports became financially less attractive to the grain users. Today an average cereal harvest in England will cover over eight million acres and yield up to twenty-six million tonnes of grain.

The three major cereal crops that have consistently been grown in England are wheat, barley and oats: over the years the wheat acreage has increased at the expense of oats. Since the war the oat acreage has fallen from over three million acres, larger than the wheat acreage, to only a quarter of a million acres today, and oat yields are still less than two tonnes to the acre. New varieties of oats may well reverse this trend with higher yields, easier harvesting and better quality.

The production of barley has increased during this period from under two million acres grown, yielding about one tonne an acre, to five million acres now producing an average of two tonnes to the acre.

Wheat production, however, has grown dramatically from one-and-a-quarter tonnes an acre on less than two-and-a-half million acres to an average yield of nearly three tonnes from five million acres. Our top wheat growers expect more than

Cultivating in Oxfordshire: After the grain has been harvested in the autumn a farmer will rip the soil with a cultivator to encourage weeds to grow. The weeds will subsequently be killed either by ploughing or by further cultivation. A medium-sized tractor with a ten-foot-wide heavy tine cultivator is able to work upwards of an acre an hour—but subsequent cultivations may well be done at twice this speed.

One of the problems associated with post-harvest stubble cultivations is that the resulting condition of the ground makes it difficult to obtain tractor wheel grip in wet weather. If the harvest has been delayed by bad weather then the time lapse between the harvest and sowing the following crop is so short that there will be too little time left for weeds to germinate in the cultivated land. An example of this particular problem is when oil seed rape drilling is following a delayed winter barley crop: in such cases farmers will forego cultivating but ensure that they make a very good job of ploughing the barley stubble, using carefully set skimmers on the plough, which will encourage the surface weeds to fall to the bottom of the plough furrow thus burying them some eight inches deep to certain death.

four tonnes of wheat from every acre of their Grades 1 and 2 land.

The nationwide increase in cereal production has, almost as a by-product, given rise to two of the most vocal and recurring criticisms directed against farmers: first, there has been the enlargement of fields by the removal of hedgerows to enable the more efficient use of ever larger tractors and combine harvesters. It has to be acknowledged that in the past thirty years in a few parts of England, particularly in East Anglia, hedgerow destruction has been overdone. Today even the most ardent expansionist accepts that there is but little benefit of scale once a field is of some fifty or so acres.

And the other major criticism directed at arable farmers is as a result of a minority of farmers who handled their burning of straw in an irresponsible manner. It is generally accepted that an effective burn of straw and stubble is worth an extra quarter of a tonne of grain an acre, and, with straw itself virtually unsaleable in many arable areas, it makes economic sense to burn the maximum amount possible and forty per cent of the straw produced is being burned. However, the farming industry itself took the lead in mitigating this problem and brought in a code of practice that was subsequently given the force of law. Today the practice of straw-burning causes the minimum of offence and provides a vital cleansing action for the soil. Straw and stubble burning will continue until such time as an economic use, such as turning straw into an industrial product, can be found, or until the practice is banned by law.

Research is being carried out in many parts of the world to find economic uses for the vast amounts of straw which are produced but, so far, little positive has resulted. The bulky nature of the product makes transporting expensive and even the use of it by farmers in their home central heating systems has proved relatively unpopular.

Ring-rolling: Ring-rolling is the final cultivation that is carried out in the spring, after ploughing, sowing and harrowing. The ring-roller not only breaks down the clods but consolidates the surface of the ground, helping to lessen moisture loss from the surface of the field.

Depending upon the type of soil involved the number of operations between two harvests on any one field will vary from perhaps only nine—in the case of light, easily worked soil—to double this number on more difficult land, with many variations in between. On easy land the stubble may be cultivated, ploughed (or cultivated twice more), harrowed, combine drilled with seed and fertiliser, harrowed and rolled, rolled again, sprayed and then combined. With difficult heavy land the stubble will be cultivated, ploughed, harrowed three times, perhaps rolled, fertilised, harrowed, drilled, harrowed, rolled and perhaps rolled again, sprayed up to four times and then harvested—all the groundwork cultivations being slower and having to be done using heavier equipment than is needed on lighter land.

In all, the number of tractor hours needed for every acre of cereals grown will vary between six and fourteen, plus the combining time.

During the 1950s and the early 1960s there was a strong movement towards cereal monoculture with a continuous planting of either wheat or barley year after year. There was a lower yield barrier which, once broken through, allowed the crop to be grown consistently at a yield commensurate with the quality of the land. It was not unusual to find farms where barley had been grown consecutively for more than twenty years. Grass weeds were often a problem resulting from monoculture and when sprays became available to overcome this it was found that the additional expense of the sprays made the enterprise unprofitable and monoculture virtually ceased except in very limited areas.

Pressures increased on farmers to produce more food and the ever higher yielding varieties of corn responded better to some form of crop rotation, however simple. The traditional rotational break crops had been potatoes, sugar beet and beans,

depending upon soil types, but it was the increase in the price available for oil seed rape in the mid-1970s which encouraged an explosion in the growing of this crop. Oil seed rape provided a good break for cereals and could be grown and harvested with conventional grain equipment. It was first grown in England in the late 1960s, but it was not until Britain's entry into the European Community, when rape prices increased significantly, that large areas of England were planted with oil seed rape, thereby adding a brilliant yellow to the tapestry of our countryside in May when the rape bears its blossom.

The tonnage produced has seen a phenomenal rise from ten thousand tonnes in 1970 to nearly a million tonnes, from seven hundred thousand acres, today. Regrettably this crop is now in considerable surplus, by over thirty per cent, and the inevitable reduction in the price of the end product will make it much less attractive to the farmer.

Potato Harvesting: During the Second World War nearly one and a half million acres of potatoes were grown; all, of course, were harvested by hand and all were consumed fresh. Today the acreage of main crop potatoes is down to 324,000 acres, each acre yielding about fifteen tonnes: virtually all are harvested by machine. A quarter of the potato acreage is now irrigated and a quarter of the total tonnage harvested goes for processing into crisps, chips and similar. All maincrop potatoes are grown under quota which is currently worth £1000 an acre.

In all, the English potato grower is satisfying eighty-six per cent of the home market: this has been a fairly constant figure over the past twenty years. About ten per cent of all potatoes grown are retained for seed, while a

further six per cent are used for feeding stock or are wasted. The early potato crop is not a significant part of the English crop: early potatoes are only grown in Cornwall and southern England, on the good lands around the Chichester plain. A good yield of 'earlies' in early June will be about eight tonnes an acre and will fetch about £500 a tonne. As the season progresses yields will increase and prices will fall, maintaining a constant gross return of about £4000 an acre. Main crop potatoes can yield up to twenty tonnes an acre harvested in late autumn and worth £46 a tonne. If growers wish to obtain the higher prices by keeping them through until the following spring then they will need to invest in a specialist storage building, costing some £100 for every tonne stored.

In 1973 oil seed rape was worth £33 a tonne; in 1986 it fetched £330: this year's harvest price will probably be below £220 a tonne and the price will continue to fall until the acreage grown is reduced to the amount the market needs.

As far as the other break crops are concerned technological advances in potato growing have resulted in a large increase in output per acre. Seven hundred thousand acres of potatoes grown twenty years ago produced an average of ten tonnes an acre: last year four-hundred-and-fifty thousand acres produced nearly fifteen tonnes for every acre. England is still less than ninety per cent self-sufficient in potatoes and improvements in management and technical details will encourage greater production here.

As economic pressures bear ever more heavily, the farmer seeks all possible ways of increasing his efficiency. Making fuller use of modern plant breeding techniques, improving the skills of his staff by further training, better management of his resources (and indeed of himself) are all being explored and implemented.

Corn Fields near Norwich: The flat lands of this area, where any rise of ten feet or more is considered to be a hill, are a major cereal producing part of England. The coming of drainage allowed the change of large areas of this countryside from waterlogged grass fields to high-yielding corn fields since the land is intrinsically of good quality over most of the county.

Norfolk is one of the more sparsely populated counties of England with an acre of land for every two people (compared with Essex with three times this density) and has, by dint of its largely favourable soils, always been a

In arable farming one of the heaviest costs is that relating to power and machinery. This cost now accounts for over forty per cent of the arable farmer's 'fixed costs' and amounts to £100 for every acre farmed: as a comparison his hired labour will cost £70 an acre and his rent £50. Arable farmers are seeking ways of reducing this heavy commitment and the smaller farmer is turning more and more to agricultural contractors for more than just specialist operations. Indeed some are handing over the major part of their machinery operations on a contract basis.

Machinery manufacturers and dealers are now entering the equipment and tractor rental field and this may well develop into there being specialist dealers who will hire out agricultural equipment, as happens in other industries.

Machinery sharing between farmers has never proved popular in England, the excuse being that they would all need the machinery involved at the same moment, which is, of course, a valid point. But as financial pressures increase still further perhaps more farmers will consider machinery sharing as a

heavily agricultural area with more people working in agriculture than in other lowland counties.

With improving road and rail communications the county is becoming a popular area for weekenders as well as holiday-makers. Farmers are realising that a surplus cottage which was worth about £20,000 only five years ago may fetch over five times that amount today. Many farmers here are also creating holiday-based ventures to cater for these blossoming needs.

viable exercise to reduce their capital investment.

There was a marked annual increase in the yield of sugar beet until 1960, which doubled its output an acre over thirty years as a result of improved varieties, earlier sowing, better fertiliser usage and disease control.

Since the 1960s there has been little further increase in yield. In 1968 four hundred and fifty thousand acres of sugar beet produced fourteen tonnes an acre, while last year half a million acres (on fourteen thousand farms) showed but a small increase in yield to sixteen tonnes an acre. However there has been a slow but sure increase in the percentage of sugar content in the beet.

Enjoying a modest revival as break crops are field peas and beans, grown mainly for combining as animal feed. The area grown of each crop is around a quarter of a million acres and both will yield about a tonne and a quarter to the acre and both will receive nearly the same price per tonne, although peas may fetch up to ten per cent more than beans. Both these crops are as financially viable as oil seed rape but they do suffer from a higher weather risk. It is probable that the area of both crops grown will increase as oil seed rape returns are reduced.

Other crops grown for harvesting as fodder crops—maize, turnips, swedes, fodder beet and mangolds—are not really significant as their total area amounts to only 125,000 acres.

On suitable land, well drained, good quality and easily worked, field scale vegetables are being grown more and more as an increasingly valuable crop. Cabbage, sprouts, green peas, carrots and cauliflowers are the mainstay of the vegetable growers taking up over eighty per cent of the total vegetable area grown of 250,000 acres.

Another fifty thousand acres are devoted to small fruit (for example, strawberries, blackcurrants and raspberries), hardy

Cauliflower Grading in Lincolnshire: Twenty-eight thousand acres of cauliflowers are grown in England with a gross output of nearly two hundred million heads. The supermarkets require small top-quality heads, which necessitates careful picking and grading. At times of the year when there is overproduction some growers open their fields to allow people to 'pick-your-own' and fix a price of, say, five for £1. Obviously, human nature being what it is, the public then pick the largest they can find leaving the smaller ones, which are the most suitable for marketing or processing, for the farmer to market in the normal way.

The way to control the size of the cauliflower is by planting a particular seed population—the greater the number of plants to the acre, the smaller will be the cauliflower. But variations in weather can play havoc with even the most meticulous planning. Irrigation of all field vegetables enables the grower to control the enterprise better, but the costs can be considerable although they vary widely depending upon water source, type of equipment used, etc. For example, a self-propelled irrigator, capable of covering fifty acres in a day in a ten-day cycle and operating for twenty-two hours a day with two moves will cost £9000. A centre-pivot sprinkler system, capable of covering one-hundred-and-thirty acres with two inches of water (which is two hundred tonnes an acre) in any period of time from one day onwards, will cost £80,000.

nursery stock, flowers and bulbs, this latter crop now accounting for ten thousand acres. Hop fields account for a further 12,500 acres.

*

As technological improvements gain ground it is becoming more and more difficult for farmers to keep pace with these developments. Spray chemicals are a classic example of where the pace of change is so rapid that it requires specialist knowledge of a very high standard to keep up with the latest chemicals and their best methods of use. Groups of like-minded farmers are getting together and employing their own agronomist to walk their fields and advise them on spraying and other relevant matters. The progressive farmer accepts the need for this type of specialist advice and considers it a good investment.

But now the major problem facing arable farmers in England is not technical, it is not even the weather (although the excessively wet harvest of 1987 dealt a severe shock to those who were complacent about weather risk), it is the apparent lack of political will amongst the leaders of the western world to stop the gross over production of so many crops and at the same time ensure the viability of their rural communities.

Many million acres of farmland have been turned over to producing these crops now in surplus because of government encouragement and the relatively higher prices received for arable crops over livestock products. In England wheat is in twenty per cent excess production, oil seed rape twenty-five per cent in excess and barley over fifty per cent. In the European Community as a whole the position is even more serious and it is estimated that at the present rate of production there could well be a surplus of cereals in excess of one hundred million tonnes by 1990 unless stringent measures are taken as a matter of urgency to control this over-production. The USA, too, is doing little to encourage their farmers to alter their land use to reduce the surpluses.

To exacerbate the situation the plant breeding scientists are on the brink of technological progress that will increase the yields of many crops in a significant manner. Possibly, as a

Onion Packing in Lincolnshire: As a direct result of better varieties, improved management and consistent marketing pressure, the acreage of onions grown has increased in twenty-five years from less than two thousand acres to over twenty-one thousand acres today, each acre yielding up to fourteen tonnes. Because of their grading, quality and storage capability English onions can satisfy the home demand throughout the year.

Main crop bulb onions are drilled from February to April and are harvested from August onwards. These onions can then be dried and stored until the following May. Winter-hardy varieties of onion, originally grown in Japan, can be sown in August and be ready for harvesting ten months later. Salad onions account for just under twenty per cent of the total onion acreage grown. The price that the grower will receive for his crop is around £100 a ton on average. The harvesting, storing and subsequent grading of onions is a highly skilled operation if the best results are to be obtained.

The Wrekin, Shropshire

result of the implementation of this successful research, we may soon see an annual increase in yield of nearer six per cent rather than the previous three per cent.

In the absence of economic markets for these surpluses, such as conversion to fuel and other industrial uses, the only way to alleviate this problem is to remove large tracts of land from producing food. The problem then facing the farmer, the politician, and indeed all those who are concerned with the future of the countryside, is what use is to be made of these acres to ensure that the rural scene remains acceptable and the rural population viable as an economic entity.

Grain Harvesting in Norfolk: Gone are the picturesque binders, the sheaves and the stooks. Massive combine harvesters (costing up to £85,000 each) are capable of cutting and threshing up to five acres an hour.

A good wheat grower will be disappointed if he fails to harvest less than three-and-a-half tonnes from every acre. The harvesting of the crop is now so mechanised that it is one of the least demanding operations on the arable farm, unless the harvesting conditions of 1987 are to become the norm.

Ideally the wheat will be cut in early August with a moisture content of less than fourteen per cent to obviate the need for artificial drying—this seldom happens. In a 'normal' year the farmer will expect to have to dry at least half his crop, and to remove up to six per cent moisture will cost £10 a tonne of grain. But to achieve this the farmer will have to invest up to £150 in capital costs for every tonne for which he requires space—forty-six cubic feet of storage for every tonne.

Stubble Burning: Forty per cent of all the straw left behind the combine harvester is now burnt. Quite rightly there are strong laws governing the timing and limitations on straw and stubble burning and farmers today appreciate the need for care and vigilance to ensure minimum inconvenience to country dwellers and users and to mitigate the potential damage to wildlife. Straw burning must not be carried out at weekends, nor on public holidays, and no fires may be left burning at night: there must always be sufficient attendants present during burning and the fires must not be left unsupervised or in the care of a minor. Headland straw must be cleared away and this area ploughed so that there is a fire break before the edge of the field. Burning should be done against the wind and the greatest care must be exercised at all times.

Straw burning will only end if it should be banned by law—and this would cause a major financial and physical problem for farmers—or if a sound commercial use could be found for the straw that is produced surplus to the feeding and bedding requirements of livestock.

Forestry

FORESTRY is most probably the best recorded land-use industry in England. For nearly a thousand years careful records have been kept of tree plantings and the eventual use that was made of the resulting timber. Also, the ways in which the forest lands were utilised have been carefully documented.

In early times the term 'forest' included all those lands, even open land, over which the kings hunted.

King Canute, in 1016 AD, was a keen tree planter and his enthusiasm was continued by William the Conqueror. In 1079 AD William I organised the planting of the New Forest for his own pleasures, especially the hunting of wild boar, and the trees when mature were used as timber for ship building.

Throughout the middle ages, kings and governments pre-served and protected the ever-expanding forests both practically and with frequent Acts of Parliament. During the seventeenth century, for example, some nine Acts went on to the statute books, including the famous Act of 1601 'to avoid and prevent divers misdemeanours in our forests by lewd and idle persons'. The mind boggles.

It was only in 1776 that the Scots Pine was introduced into the New Forest, the first time this species had been cultivated in England.

Gradually the requirements of the naval shipbuilders denuded the countryside of the trees required for their vessels, and today England has only two million acres, or less than seven per cent of its land surface, afforested.

A Bluebell Wood in Gloucestershire: An all too rare sight as intensive farming systems have removed many commercially unproductive woodlands where bluebells thrive. Today the realisation of the need for conservation and the less attractive prospect for cereal growing should ensure the survival of those bluebell woods that remain, especially with the added emphasis of the need for better access to the countryside for visitors. Slowly but surely all those who are concerned for the future of the countryside are getting together and speaking the same language. The extremists, on both sides, are becoming isolated, and intelligent, positive dialogue is taking place instead of confrontation. Farmers are prepared to be guided now that it is reasonably clear what is required. Regrettably, in some areas, it is the planners who are inhibiting sensible development and preventing farmers from converting unused, often derelict and unsightly, farm buildings into worthwhile dwellings or workshops. Edicts may be issued from the various governmental bodies, but it is usually the local planners who have the final say and too many are opting for stagnation rather than conservation.

As the need for timber for shipbuilding diminished many forest areas were planted with the faster growing coniferous trees so that today they account for nearly half the English woodland areas. The trend to conifers was accelerated when, in 1919, the Forestry Commission was set up by an Act of Parliament. This Act followed the great forestry debates of the previous sixty years during which time there were six Royal Commissions and Select Committees all of which achieved little. Forestry was a neglected industry and it was not until the timber shortages of the First World War that the need for a genuine forestry policy was brought home to those in power.

At the beginning of the First World War some eleven million cubic metres of unprocessed timber was being imported into England every year. The blockade of seaways restricted these imports and as a result over 450,000 acres of forest in Great Britain were felled in those five years of war.

The powers given to the Forestry Commission in 1919 were considerable. They included the power to buy, to acquire and to dispose of standing timber, and, most importantly of all, to make grants or loans to encourage timber planting and production. Also the training of forestry workers, as well as timber research, was brought under the aegis of the Forestry Commission. The intention was to reafforest nearly two million acres of land in Great Britain.

The post-war depression of 1921 led to an all out effort by the Forestry Commission to recruit more forestry workers to help to relieve the increasing unemployment problem. Soon, however, serious financial deficits almost led to the disappearance of the Commission into the Ministry of Agriculture. This unhappy situation was averted largely as a result of the personal efforts of Lord Lovat, the Chairman of the Commission at that time. The Commission's position was consolidated in 1923 when all the Crown forests were transferred to the Commission's responsibility and it became the sole forest authority.

The planting that took place was not productive enough to

Woodlands: Although less than seven per cent of England is afforested, in most areas woodland trees provide an aesthetic backcloth to the farmers' 'factory floor'. In the 1960s and the early 70s the foresters in a few upland areas, both privately owned and owned by the Forestry Commission, committed land to the widely considered visual crime of blanket spruce planting over large areas of hillside. With no imagination and ignoring the possibility of using different species to soften and improve the image whole forests of spruce were created, causing conflict with all and sundry. Now the ash, the beech, the birch, the oak, the fir, the larch and various pines are planted together to improve the scene: and simultaneously better siting is practised so that the modern forest will be better both visually and environmentally. Since England is minimally afforested there is plenty of need for more forest planting and the recent government scheme for farm woodland grants should encourage a number of farmers to plant a considerable acreage into trees over the next ten years.

relieve the need for considerable imports, and by the outbreak of the Second World War in 1939 some ninety-six per cent of the timber needs of the country were being imported. Large areas of forest were thus once again felled as vital imports of food took precedence over the importing of timber: the total area of woodland felled during the Second World War in Great Britain was over half a million acres, which meant that all worthwhile timber was cut.

By 1957 it was at last realised, at least by the Zuckerman Committee investigating the future of the country's national resources, that forestry not only stood economically in its own right, but had a part to play in improving the environment and providing leisure activities, and could provide a worthwhile integration with farming.

A forest census in 1966 showed that there were two-and-a-quarter million acres of forest land in England, much of it in a poor state of management.

The boom years of farming in the 1970s meant that land prices in England increased dramatically from an average of £250 an acre in 1970 to £1750 an acre by 1979, which effectively ruled out economic woodland planting on this land. Government itself felt that the need for more afforestation had been overstated and recommended that fewer areas be planted, and, sensibly, that more thought be given to enhancing the appearance of woodland and more emphasis be placed on the recreational use of the Forestry Commission forests.

Favourable fiscal legislation led to forest activity increasing in both Scotland and Wales during the 1970s, where the uplands could be purchased more cheaply than in England, but not until 1981 were all the grant schemes brought into one Forestry Grant Scheme and at the same time it was agreed that Forestry Commission land should be sold to the private sector of forestry. Gradually had come the realisation that, aesthetically at least, mixed forests of hardwoods and conifers were preferable to solely conifer woodlands, and planting grants for broad-leaved species were increased.

A Timber Yard: There are many small timber yards which provide a vital service to woodland owners right across England. The economic future of these small yards, if they are efficient, looks secure, since, with increasing government support, it is likely that the acreage of trees being planted in England will continue to grow at an ever increasing pace. Alongside new plantings must come the improvement of existing, currently unmanaged, woodlands. Of the total 115,000 acres of broadleaved woods in England, probably two-thirds could be categorised in this way. The problem is that the average acreage of woodland on each farm in England that has woods at all is only fifteen acres, which is too small to be commercially viable: but with the new grants for woodland improvement farmers will take a new look at their trees and their subsequent improvement will add to the beauty of the countryside.

Forestry, in all its forms, is set to become the new growth industry and this is to be welcomed not least for the extra jobs it will create—every three hundred acres of forestry means one full-time job.

plantation

By 1986 it was realised that the increase in the output of food from many of the acres in England had to be reduced and that a significant percentage of this land had to be removed from food production altogether. For the first time in our history landowners, and tenants too, were offered significant guaranteed annual sums for up to forty years to plant up their land with broad-leaved forests, for thirty years for mixed forests and for twenty years for conifers. These annual payments were to be made in addition to the existing planting grants with the aim of making timber production a feasible economic alternative to food production.

It is now considered that England alone needs to remove three million acres from food production if a supply and demand balance is to be achieved and that one million of these acres could be afforested with significant social and environmental gain. Farmers have to be convinced, however, that the annual grants proposed will be kept in reasonable pace with inflation and that there will still be a demand for the timber when it is mature. It is inevitable that if sufficient increases in plantings do take place then not only will this slow the decline in rural employment (for one man is needed for every three hundred acres of wood) but it will also mean growth in timber-based industries.

Of the four major sources of energy, wood, coal, oil and gas,

only wood is constantly renewable, and so the increase in forest land will increase our energy reserves as well as improve the general environment.

The first hurricane in England for over two hundred years caused frightening chaos and terrible destruction to the south-eastern quarter of England. It is estimated that the 120-miles-per-hour winds destroyed over twenty million trees and damaged even more. Whole plantations were smashed, wood-lands decimated and hedgerow trees felled like ninepins.

Large landscapes have changed and it will take a long time for all the fallen trees to be dealt with. Replanting, where considered sensible, combined with the extra planting as a result of the new government support for amenity woodlands, will create an enormous demand for saplings and seedlings—a challenge for forest nurseries.

The quantities of timber that were made available by the storm damage highlighted the need for more localised timber processing works and it is to be hoped that this side of the forestry industry will be able to keep pace with the pressures that are being put upon it.

Alternative Livestock & Cropping

THERE are a variety of new animal enterprises that could be developed in an economic manner in England and thus provide either import replacements, an export demand or meet a growing home demand.

In the first category, that of import replacement, is rabbit farming, the development of finer wool from sheep and from goats, and the rearing of deer for venison. Perhaps the enterprise with the greatest potential here is the breeding of goats for the production of both angora and cashmere fibre. There is an ever-increasing demand for fabrics containing cashmere and angora and there is a world shortage which is causing rapid price increases. It would take at least five years for sufficient foundation stock to be imported and then bred here, and there would also be a need for people trained in the handling of these animals and with experience in the production of the fibre. Once the home market was satisfied then there would remain a large export demand for these high quality products.

There is an increasing home demand for goats' milk for both the organic and specialist medical markets. Unfortunately the current level of both goat breeding and management expertise is relatively low when compared to dairying and it will be many years before economic yields can be seen from anything but the very smallest herds.

As far as existing livestock enterprises are concerned, there is considerable scope for expansion in the horse field, for turkeys and for outdoor pigs. The additional advantage of increasing the number of livestock, of all sorts, is that they create an additional demand for feed crops and in all perhaps one million additional acres would have to be devoted to their needs.

Horseyculture: It is possible for well-kept horse paddocks to contribute to the beauty of the rural scene, but too often old oil drums, broken fences and weed-infested meadows are their signature. It is important that horse owners appreciate how easy and how necessary it is to take a pride in their horse paddocks if we are to see a further large acreage handed over to their use.

Before the advent of the tractor the vast majority of horses were working horses (there are now fewer than twelve thousand heavy horses, all kept for pleasure or for ploughing demonstrations) but now it is estimated that there are over half a million horses in England kept for recreational purposes. Horse riding is one of our fastest growing hobby pursuits and the provision of both grazing and other feed requirements will provide considerable, and profitable, supplementary income for farmers. It could utilise up to half a million acres.

Although deer have roamed wild over large parts of England for centuries it is only in the last few years that they have actually been farmed. The Fallow, the Roe and the Muntjac are far more numerous than most casual observers of the countryside are aware. Farmers need to cull these breeds selectively on a regular basis to ensure their survival and also to mitigate the damage they can cause to agricultural and horticultural crops (not to mention gardens—roses being a speciality) if allowed to breed unchecked. The sale of venison from the culling operation can make a small contribution to farm income.

It is the Red Deer that is being farmed in ever increasing numbers. Already there are more than one hundred and fifty Red Deer farms with a total of over ten thousand hinds being kept for breeding. Careful selection and culling of breeding stock is ensuring a continual improvement in the suitability of these animals for intensive venison production. Apart from the production of meat there is a growing demand for English bred stags and hinds throughout the world and a significant export trade in live animals is growing.

The initial cost of establishing a herd is very high, involving amongst other things very expensive fencing, and so it will be only those with both the enthusiasm and the large amount of capital necessary who will be able to exploit this new enterprise in farming. Deer farming can make a useful, albeit small and selective, contribution to providing an alternative livestock enterprise for some English farmers.

A significant increase in the number of horses kept could be achieved by conferring upon the horse 'agricultural status' so that they would be treated for tax purposes, and indeed rating, as other livestock. Up to a further half a million acres could easily be taken up in this way and at the same time the horses would create a large demand for additional rural employment.

There is a great need for more research and development into all these aspects of alternative livestock enterprises if they are to be expanded sufficiently to create economically viable industries in their own right and not, as is so often the case, be merely hobby activities.

*

Horse Ploughing: Perhaps the greatest attraction at ploughing matches or agricultural shows is the demonstration of ploughing by the heavy horses. There are still in England ten thousand Shires, some seven hundred Clydesdales and a further thousand heavy horses of other breeds, such as Suffolks and Percherons: these are mainly kept for demonstrations and recreational purposes.

It is very unusual to find any farms today which use horses for farmwork unless it is for sentimental or nostalgic reasons. It was suggested during the 1974 oil price explosion that 'farmers will return to the practice of keeping working horses in order to eke out expensive tractor fuel'. But this is probably as likely as the average Englishman giving up his car and returning to the horse and buggy—highly picturesque but somewhat impractical.

The most obvious expansion of alternative cropping is for the planting of a further one million acres of forestry, as both commercial forests and as amenity woodland. Other existing crops worthy of further acreage are linseed, durum wheat, winter brassicas, peas and pot plants. New crops, or at least crops that are at present grown in insignificant amounts but which could be grown over a larger area, include flax, soft fruits, essential and medicinal oils, new salad crops, herbs, chickpeas, lentils, navy beans, sunflowers, high-lysine cereals, protein beets, oil peas, lupins and flowerseeds.

Hops were once grown right across England for many hundreds of years. Almost every town, and many villages, boasted its own brewery, and the demand for hops was so great that in 1885 71,327 acres were grown.

As brewing became more centralised hop growing developed around three areas, Kent and Sussex, Worcestershire and Herefordshire, and a smaller area in Hampshire. By 1980 the demands of the beer drinking public changed to the lager-type beers for which the English hop was less suitable. Demand for English hops fell and the price dropped rapidly from a peak of £3600 a tonne in 1984 to £2460 in 1987.

The acreage grown declined in line with the price fall from nearly fifteen thousand acres in 1980 to only twelve-and-a-half thousand in 1987, but the industry has now researched and developed new seedless varieties able to produce good yields and also attractive to overseas brewers. Two new varieties, Yeoman and Target, appear to fill this slot and it is anticipated that the acreage of hops grown will increase by over fifty per cent in the next ten years thus providing an alternative economic land-use for a number of farmers in the favoured hop growing areas. With the exception of linseed, which could well be economically grown over a million acres of land in England, none of the above crops could individually cover a great acreage, but taken together they could make a substantial contribution to the profitability of farming as a whole.

As with livestock, there is a great need for more research into the growing of these crops to enable them to become viable substitutes for conventional food production and at the same time enhance the rural scene and provide more rural employment.

With the planting of more forests and the growing of more linseed all the alternative crops grown could well, within ten

Longhorns: Rare breeds are maintained on some farms not only for their scenic and rarity value but also to provide a long-term gene bank to meet possible future breeding needs.

The small number of people who are contributing to our heritage in this manner deserve support for their enthusiasm for they are providing a useful service. In some places large numbers of rare breeds of many species have been brought together and are on view to the public. Most, though, are kept on small holdings because of personal preference, or some might say the idiosyncracy, of the owner.

years, amount to an additional three million acres of land being used usefully and economically to provide a sensible alternative to cereals.

There is also a growing demand for more and better garden and house plants and farm based garden centres are making a useful return from exploiting this demand.

Greenhouses are being developed and modernised to meet the increasing demand for their output. Of the 5300 acres of greenhouses in England over two-thirds are fitted with heating equipment and can thus control the seasonality and production of their crops.

Vegetables, mainly tomatoes, occupy 2750 acres of these glasshouses, while the remainder produce flowers and plants. This is a growing business and can make a contribution to the farming industry's income by adding value to its products.

A relatively new business in the countryside is the farm shop, often combined with a 'pick your own' operation. Over several parts of the country enlightened councils have given planning permission to farmers to sell their produce directly to the public, thus saving on transport, handling and middlemen costs to the benefit of both the farmer and the consumer. In many cases farmers have expanded these farm shops to sell garden requisites and other allied products not necessarily produced on their own farms.

'Pick your own' fruit and vegetable farms are extremely popular since they provide whole families with a good reason to get out into the countryside to procure varied and fresh produce usually at a lower price than in the shops. Provided that the enterprise is well managed and the various needs of customers well catered for 'pick your own' provides a useful income for the grower while at the same time familiarising the layman with the ways of the countryside.

*

A Longhorn Bull in Gloucestershire: Although the history of Longhorn cattle can be traced back to before the time of William the Conqueror it was not until the mid-1750s that the fixation of specific breeds of cattle in England began. Indeed in 1780 some of Bakewell's Longhorns were exported to Scotland for crossing with the local indigenous cattle of that time, the West Highland and the Banffshire.

Today the Longhorn is no more than an indulgent reminder of times past for genetic improvement of the beef breeds has rendered it superfluous to modern needs. The beef animal today has to be a fast growing, even tempered, domesticated animal which produces meat that is easily recognised and easily jointed and with a minimum of fat. Even the more recent British breeds like the Hereford and the Angus are only now beginning to fight back against the foreign invasion by the Charolais, the Limousin, the Simmental and very recently the Belgian Blue, which have all out-performed them over the past fifteen years.

The production of energy from cereals, sugar and forest products is a long term possibility. At the present cost of producing energy from oil the conversion of these products is not an economic proposition, since it currently costs, for example, nearly three times as much to obtain gigajoules of energy from sugar beet as it does from oil. However, the time may come when the world's oil reservoirs become depleted and the cost of oil increases—then the production of energy from farm grown materials might become a viable proposition. If oil were £16 a barrel and wheat were £50 a tonne then conversion would be an economic proposition.

Our government must, therefore, encourage more research in this area for, unlike oil, cereals, sugar and forest products are all renewable resources.

A great deal of thought and effort has to be put into finding viable alternative uses for the areas of land to be removed from food production.

If England's agricultural productivity should rise by just two per cent a year (and past history shows that this could well happen), and if at the same time population growth remains constant, then more than half the present cereal acreage will have to be taken out of producing grain by soon after the turn of the century. Similarly, since there will have to be big reductions in the number of livestock kept, the food-producing grassland acreage will have to be cut by about a quarter. This means that within the next twenty-year period alternative economic non-food producing uses will have to be found for over six million acres of land. This is a challenge which I am sure England's farmers will meet if they are given a lead and also encouragement by government.

Deer Farming: It takes a beef calf around forty-seven days to double its birth weight, but a deer calf will double its birth weight in less than twenty days.

It is the Red Deer which is intensively farmed, while Fallow Deer are mainly kept for their ornamental qualities, although their meat can provide a small but useful income.

Deer farming is currently at the same stage of development as was pig farming fifty years ago: it is a cottage industry. Its growth will depend ultimately upon the success or otherwise that deer farmers make of marketing their end product, venison. Everything connected with setting up a deer farm is expensive. A thirty-five acre field, necessary for a hundred head herd, will need, on average, more than two thousand yards of six-foot-high fencing, costing £3 a yard. A minimum building requirement is for three thousand square feet which would cost £25,000: handling equipment would add a further £3000. One hundred hinds and the necessary four stags would cost at least £40,000. This makes a grand total of £80,000 if one includes £6000 for working capital—a daunting investment. If venison can be marketed and sold by the producer for not less than £1.40 a pound then it is commercially viable—just. Only time will tell, but if the quality of the marketing can be ensured then deer farming will provide a useful alternative livestock enterprise largely free from political pressures for a few farmers.

Alternative Land-Use

GRADUALLY landowners and farmers are accepting the fact that they do not have to be solely food producers to be content and successful. Indeed a significant minority of farmers now recognise that there is a large market, largely untapped, for leisure activities in the countryside and that there are economically viable uses for their farms, or parts of them, other than that of producing food.

More and more the affluent, mainly urban, society feels the need to get out into the pure air of the countryside to enjoy themselves with their families and friends. This wish now extends beyond the annual holiday and weekends and the countryside acts as a magnet to many city dwellers throughout the year.

Many farmhouses and redundant farm buildings are being converted, with far-sighted local authority approval, into guest-house accommodation: redundant cottages, in any case often unsuitable for farm employees, are being sold as second homes. Carefully sited caravan and camping sites are being established along with the necessary on-site facilities—restaurants, showers, shops and places of entertainment.

Some farmers are entering the specialised holiday field catering for field study groups—artists, fishermen and those who shoot. A keen Hampshire farmer and conservationist recently said, 'Many people do not wish to kill anything, but they should recognise that man will go to great lengths to preserve his prey, for to kill the last one is to hunt no more.' Similarly a leading

Shooting in Norfolk: More and more farmers are realising the value of providing those who wish to shoot with a suitable environment. The supply of wild birds is augmented by the rearing of game birds in captivity and subsequently releasing them: pheasant and partridge adapt readily to farmland, but grouse do not. There is pressure from conservationists for farmers to leave their cereal land headlands unsprayed by chemicals for a distance of 20 feet. This would provide an excellent habitat for wild birds and surprisingly would have little adverse effect on the overall yield of grain.

Pheasants and partridges are the main game birds on lowland farms with the occasional snipe and woodcock, while rabbits and hares can add to the bag. Where there are suitable ponds, and over two thousand new farm ponds are being dug every year, then duck shooting can be an added attraction to those who enjoy shooting. The planting of new copses and the management of existing woodland enhance the attraction of the shoot, as would judicious planting of specialist cover crops for the birds. The costs of maintaining a shoot are considerable, especially since a thousand acre shoot will need one full-time gamekeeper. This shoot will, if properly run, provide some ten days of shooting for eight guns each season.

Recent Game Conservancy figures suggest that the average cost is in excess of £14 per pheasant shot on owned lowland shoots.

European ornithologist wrote, 'Whilst I disapprove in principle of these sporting activities, their side effects are so beneficial to wild life that in practice I cannot but be a supporter of field sports. It would be unrealistic to expect our countryside to be maintained in a remotely comparable fashion by landowners fired solely by altruism rather than sporting or financial considerations.'

Horse based activities are growing with centres being set up for trekking, eventing, polo, hunting, livery and grazing; also equestrian centres and clubs.

Farm trails, wildlife parks and farms catering for a large number of paying visitors, are also contributing to rural prosperity: and new rural-based centres for specific sporting activities, such as golf, tennis, squash and athletics, are being established by landowners and farmers, who are exploiting a need and using their resources in the best way possible.

Sadly, but inevitably, there are a significant number of failures amongst those who diversify haphazardly. Some farmers, unable to see or accept the need for a complete change, both in attitude and management expertise, fail to manage the operation to their own or their customers' advantage. A change of outlook is required that is sometimes too difficult for established farmers to encompass and their endeavours are, therefore, doomed to failure.

*

Probably the most popular alternative land-use may well become the farming of land under the government sponsored Environmentally Sensitive Areas scheme. Early in 1986 five sites were designated by the Ministry of Agriculture so that 'farmers in these areas will be offered incentive payments to continue the more traditional farming methods and maintain the beauty and wildlife value of their farms'. It was suggested by the Minister that 'this new departure in agricultural policy is designed to reconcile the needs of commercial farm management with enhanced landscape and wildlife protection in important areas of the country'.

A Wildlife Park in Somerset: A few large estates have converted part of their land to accommodate large-scale wildlife parks, some attracting up to half a million paying visitors a year. The demand for more facilities for visitors to the countryside is growing and an increasing number of farmers are becoming aware of this demand and exploiting it acceptably. There is a classic example in Somerset of a large farm which has diversified in two ways simultaneously: agriculturally they have added value to the milk from their six hundred dairy cows by building up both a retail milk round in the local towns and by manufacturing real dairy ice-cream in thirteen different flavours. And, on the leisure side, in 1967 they were perceptive enough to realise that there would be a demand for a wildlife park, a country life museum, an open farm, craft workshops, woodland walks, half a mile of miniature railway, a garden, a farm produce shop and a gift shop. They have recently modernised their restaurant which now caters for private functions such as weddings as well as for the day visitors. The National Heavy Horse Centre is also based there. Visitors to the estate can have a thoroughly enjoyable day out, at the same time learning a great deal about farming, wildlife and the countryside.

The five areas chosen were the Broads in Norfolk, the Somerset Levels, the South Downs, the Pennine Dales and West Penwith in Cornwall. The total area affected is only about one per cent of England's farmland, but the response by farmers has been amazingly good with nearly sixty per cent of the total area (one-hundred-and-forty thousand acres in all) being committed to the scheme for a minimum period of five years.

For the first time grants to farmers from the government have been tied to the way in which the land is managed rather than to investments or payments designed to increase a farmer's efficiency or output.

Following the undoubted enthusiasm for a scheme which will, if only slightly, reduce food production and at the same time preserve the landscape, further ESA's were set up in England in 1988: these six extra sites were the Suffolk river valleys, the Test Valley in Hampshire, the North Peak in Derbyshire, the Clun in Shropshire and an extension to the existing ESA on the South Downs.

The payments under the Environmentally Sensitive Area schemes of guaranteed government monies depend upon whether the land that is entered is being farmed as grassland or arable land. In the former case a farmer will receive £14 an acre a year grant, for the five year management agreement period, for managing the existing grassland in an agreed way. This will usually involve limiting the stocking rate, using no artificial fertilisers, controlling the uses of pesticides, herbicides and lime, curbing drainage works and taking advice on the maintenance of hedges, dew ponds, walls, banks, reed beds, woodland and scrub. This is all to ensure that the grassland has a maximum conservation value.

If the fields involved are in arable cropping then the farmer can receive £50 an acre a year for the five year period if he puts the land back into grass and manages it in accordance with the

---

A Farm Park: Some farmers are modifying their farming operations in order to attract members of the public to part with their money to see the every-day workings of a farm: as an added attraction there may be rare breeds of livestock on view.

These farmers are not only providing a useful service in catering for the needs of the urban dwellers but they are also helping their fellow farmers by educating the public in country lore and needs. A particular farm park near Tunbridge Wells in Kent takes up less than two acres of a one-hundred-and-eighty acre fruit and arable farm. The farm park keeps both usual and unusual breeds of cows, pigs, sheep, goats, ponies, various fowls, and tries always to have young animals of these species, which are always so appealing. In addition there is a butterfly house and, perhaps its biggest contribution to farming's public relations, an information room. Bright and easy-to-read posters and samples of various seeds and plants illustrate farming life in a way that can be understood and appreciated by visitors of all ages, who, in many cases, know nothing whatsoever about farming. A farm trail, encircling the farm, expands this information in a practical way with frequent and clear explanatory notices.

ESA regulations. This higher level of grant may well be continued beyond the initial five year minimum period of commitment.

The whole of the farming industry is anxious to find out what steps government may have in store to lessen over-production of food. There is a continuing discussion of land set-aside with wide ranging debate over type and effect.

Many politicians promote the voluntary system as practised in the USA, while the realists point out that in the States a voluntary reduction of cereal acreage of twenty-seven per cent reduced production by only two per cent. American farmers obviously only set aside their poorer land and with the sub-sidies paid by the government purchased more fertiliser and thus produced more grain from the land left in cultivation. The same would happen in England were a voluntary scheme to be introduced.

A further debate concerns whether 'green fallowing' (surely a contradiction in terms?) should be allowed on the land that is to be set aside. Green fallowing would allow the planting of grass on this land, which would then inevitably lead to more production of meat from the grass-consuming beef and sheep, thereby exacerbating the over-supply problem in this sector.

But worst of all for farmers is the procrastination of all the European governments in failing to agree to some form of control. Dates when agreed schemes are to be implemented come and go with prodigious recklessness, while farmers hesitate to reduce their cereal production in case cereal quotas, similar to milk quotas, are ultimately imposed. If this were the case then those who had voluntarily reduced their production would be seriously penalised with severely reduced quotas.

The farmers of England can and do appreciate the fact that their grain production has to be curtailed, but, not unreasonably in an industry so influenced by political decisions, cannot act unilaterally until the government has shown the way in which it wishes the industry to proceed.

There is a growing minority of farmers who believe that the solution to the problem of over-production in the western world is to farm organically. This is where the farmer uses no chemicals or artificial fertilisers on his crops. He relies on careful crop rotations and cultivations to control his weeds and on farmyard manure for fertiliser.

Unfortunately the inevitably lower yields and the poorer quality (because of the attacks by pests and diseases that would normally be controlled by chemical pesticide and herbicide sprays) means that the organic farmer needs a substantial premium for the end product if he is to survive financially.

While there are sufficient people who are prepared to pay this premium for what they genuinely believe to be better, purer and more wholesome food, then a few farmers may be able to eke out a living by catering for this need. Unfortunately for the organic disciple the great majority of the public demand the cheapest food possible commensurate with the requirement that it shall be of the highest quality, both visually and gastronomically. It is the inorganic farmer who is best able to satisfy this demand.

Organic farmers will not be able to compete, either financially or with the necessary quality, and so organic farming can make only a very minor contribution to reducing the surpluses of food produced in the west.

Further action by the Government to reduce excess food production by encouraging alternative land-use has been the launching of a Farm Woodland Scheme under which farmers will be paid an annual grant: the amount and duration of the grant will depend upon the types of trees planted and the quality of the land involved. For example, a hardwood forest on good Grade 3 land qualifies for a grant of £76 an acre every year for a period of forty years in addition to the normal once only forestry planting grant of up to £400 an acre. The success of this scheme in removing land from food production may well depend upon the annual grant being index-linked for inflation.

Quite a significant area of land is also being lost to agriculture each year by the construction of much needed but unsightly motorways. This land and that used for new buildings, both residential and commercial, amounts each year to an area of more than sixty thousand acres—the size of the Isle of Wight.

The Future

ACCURATE forecasting is always difficult, but especially so when one is having to anticipate the results of actions yet to be taken by multi-national politicians. The development of rural England has always been influenced by national government decisions which have affected the prosperity and the stability of rural life. Throughout history the fluctuating fortunes of landowners and farmers, and thus all who were employed in the rural areas, has meant a constant change in the way the countryside has appeared to the on-looker. The intermittent depressions that have occurred over the centuries caused poverty and thus dereliction over large parts of rural England from time to time.

Today the countryside is once again threatened by agricultural depression largely as a result of the procrastination and indecision of the governments of the European Community.

Technology, good management and financial reward have all contributed to the current surplus production throughout the developed world. Farm land has to be taken out of producing food, and once the size of the necessary area to be removed is decided, the problem facing both the occupiers of this land, and the governments concerned, is how to use this area economically and not let it descend into dereliction and disarray and thus become neglected and unsightly.

There are strongly held views in some continental countries, notably France and Germany, that almost however much it costs their taxpayers it is vital to maintain a large working population in farming. England has never subscribed to this view and, as a result, farms in England have become mechanised at the expense of labour to such an extent that little more than two per cent of the working population are directly

The Family Farm: The economic pressures on the true family farm, which provides so much rural and social stability, have made it very difficult for them to survive, let alone prosper. The only accurate definition of a family farm is a farm where all the labour is supplied by the family and all the farming assets are family owned, be they owner-occupiers or tenants. Many family farms are situated in what are known as Less Favoured Areas (LFAs) and although they qualify for special grants they are often too small for current economic viability. England is more fortunate than most countries in having only seventeen per cent of its agricultural land in LFAs: the European Community has fifty-two per cent. The rapid loss of family farms owing to economic pressures means that the more remote rural areas are being denuded of what has traditionally been the backbone of the countryside and the farming industry. The often harsh environment of the LFAs also means that the offspring of the present farmers are less inclined to follow in their parents' footsteps and seek kindlier and more remunerative occupations.

engaged in farming. In the past twenty years the number of people employed on farms has fallen by fifty per cent. In contrast, Ireland still has thirteen per cent of its population employed in agriculture, Italy ten per cent and France seven per cent. The Mediterranean countries within the European Community, namely, Greece, Spain and Portugal all have close to thirty per cent of their population employed in farming.

The European Community of Twelve has an average farm size of twenty seven acres, one sixth of the average English farm, which exacerbates the difficulty of finding a communally acceptable mitigation of the recurring problems.

Thus to forecast what is to happen in England is far more difficult now since one must assume that Britain will not only remain within the European Community but will acquiesce to the majority view on how to cope with the over-production problem. Commonsense economics would suggest that to annul current over-production not less than twenty-five per cent of the present farm land in England will have to be removed from food production during the next twenty years, a

formidable undertaking for both the farmers and the nation, perhaps too daunting for even the most ardent reformer.

Rural England will be encouraged by financial inducements and legislation to accept that food production must be significantly reduced and that the land removed from food production must be used for alternative enterprises and must not be allowed to become derelict.

In addition, in certain areas, food production will be reduced by the implementation of the Environmentally Sensitive Areas rules, but even here the visual aspect of the land involved will be an important consideration.

Whatever governments and other experts may forecast there is nagging uncertainty in many people's minds that there may one day be another happening which could alter the whole pattern of future world food requirements. One thinks back to April 1986 when the world slowly woke up to the realisation that the name of a small town in Russia would enter the history books and become a name conveying fear and horror—Chernobyl. The results of this nuclear accident will continue to

Wensleydale: Most of the original cheese-making farms, which made famous the local names, have long since disappeared: in fact little farmhouse cheese-making remains in England today though there has been a recent revival, particularly in the south west. Many of the original dairy farms in the dales have amalgamated and are now predominantly sheep farms or providers of tourist facilities, bed and breakfast or afternoon teas.

The farmers who live in this particularly beautiful part of the country have learnt that with the difficult climate, both physical and political, they must maximise the resources that they do have. One of these is the attraction of the area for holiday makers and under the banner of 'Herriot's Yorkshire Moors and Dales' (thereby cashing in, perfectly justifiably, on a famous local name) some of them have combined their leisure marketing and sustained a successful campaign bringing to the public's attention many of the facilities that they offer, including fishing, farm trails, open farms, river rides, historic houses and, of course, good accommodation.

be felt in many parts of the world and what was at the time described as a minor mishap is a dire warning that a major mishap could mean that every available non-contaminated area would be needed to produce food once again.

In contrast to the situation in the last agricultural depression in the 1930s, when vast areas of rural England became un-farmed and run down, the nation is now very much more aware of its heritage and is determined that rural England remains both kempt and aesthetically acceptable. If it meets the needs of the nation then it will provide both stimulating and satisfy-ing occupations for its inhabitants. Leisure time is increasing and becoming more important to urban workers and they are increasingly taking a more active interest in how 'their' countryside appears to 'them'. For example, the membership of the various conservation lobbies now outnumbers the total number of farmers and landowners by more than twenty-five to one. Antipathy between these lobbies and the land occupiers is now fast becoming the exception rather than the rule. It is the extremists, on both sides, who fail to understand that mutuality of interest is more than ever of paramount import-ance. It is very much in farmers' interests to encourage this

powerful conservation lobby and this they are doing. Criticism of farmers and their supposed lack of interest in the aesthetics of the countryside is not new and much of it is ill-informed. Throughout history there has been similar criticism whenever there has been change.

Seventy years ago the well-known gardener and landscaper, Gertrude Jekyll wrote, 'If the farmer of arable land could have it all his own way, not only would hedgerow timber disappear but with it the hedge-banks themselves.'

Over the past forty years, despite what extremists may say, less than one half of one per cent of hedgerows have been removed each year over the whole of England. Walls, banks, ditches and woodland fringes to fields are virtually as plentiful today as they were at the end of the Second World War.

The facts can, however, speak for themselves. In the past five years over thirty million trees have been planted on England's farms, with more than half of them broad-leaved (i.e. hardwood). Over twenty thousand new farm ponds (making over one hundred and fifty thousand in all) have been dug and there are enough farm hedgerows to encircle the world ten times.

The Cotswolds in April: Even in the mildest of springs there can be a sudden downfall of snow. To the casual observer late snows can add a strange, almost ethereal, dimension to the beauty of the countryside, but the farmer in these conditions has to be prepared to supply extra feed to his animals even if they have been grazing for some weeks. The snows will seldom last for more than a few days, but sometimes it causes considerable stress to animals which spent the winter in sheltered housing. The additional cost of the extra food and labour involved can be a considerable burden to the Cotswold farmer whose livelihood may already be precarious.

A further indicator of farmers' enthusiasm for the preservation of all forms of wildlife in the countryside is that in every county of England there is now a Farming and Wildlife Advisory Group. These very active FWAGs are so aptly described as 'true partnerships in practical conservation between farmers and other conservationists'.

Over the years most of England's farmers and landowners have reinvested their profits in their farms so as to ensure that they remained economically viable and at the same time are able to respond to the recurrent pleas of successive governments to produce the food necessary to feed the nation.

The last two years, however, have seen a significant fall in investment in farm buildings and machinery. This indicates a lack of confidence in an industry that spends over £6500 million a year on farm requisites, and as a result generates nearly one-and-a-half million jobs, and is a serious indicator of what could happen if the present uncertainty were allowed to continue.

Farmers' incomes, in real terms, have fallen heavily in the past ten years: they will continue to do so until it is realised by both farmers and government that a significant portion of future farming incomes must come from using a proportion of the agricultural land in England in other ways than for food production. Nitrogen quotas (or taxes) and all the other negative solutions that are being put forward will never be the sensible answer to the problem. And the land that remains in food production must be farmed to its maximum economic intensity so that English farmers will be able to compete on equal terms with farmers from other countries.

If the countryside is to remain a vision acceptable to those who cherish it then it must be understood that it cannot remain so if farmers, who are the willing and proud custodians of the countryside, are impoverished. Neglected or untended land can never be a conservationist's delight and it will only be by farmers' careful and caring management that England will continue to be the green and pleasant land that we all love and enjoy.

Sunset over Warwickshire: The farmers of England have overcome many difficult situations over the years and it is hoped that the large majority will come through the present crisis, perhaps leaner and fitter. Farmers realise, and they must explain to their fellow countrymen, that the destiny of agriculture, and thus the condition of the countryside, largely rests with the political decisions that are made over the coming years.

If farmers are to make the best use of whatever resources are avaiblable to them, then the industry has the right to expect a five-year rolling strategic plan to help them plan ahead. This would enable at least some of the problems to be foreseen and the necessary remedial action taken. Once farmers know what the nation expects of them they will plan and act accordingly. Their determination and dedication will ensure that they will meet the challenge of change and do their utmost to make certain that England will remain a green and pleasant land.

Appendixes

A scheme of the Income and Expense of the several families of England, calculated for the year 1688

(From Tables of Estimates by Gregory King, Charles Davenant and W. Couling)

Number of Families	Ranks, Degrees, Titles, and Qualifications	Heads per Family	Number of Persons	Yearly Income per Family (£ s.)	Yearly Income in General (£)	Yearly Income per Head (£ s.)	Yearly Expense per Head (£ s. d.)	Yearly Increase per Head (£ s. d.)	Yearly Increase in General (£)
160	Temporal lords, - - -	40	6,400	3,200 0	512,000	80 0	70 0 0	10 0 0	64,000
26	Spiritual lords, - - -	20	520	1,300 0	33,800	65 0	45 0 0	20 0 0	10,400
800	Baronets, - - - -	10	12,800	880 0	704,000	55 0	49 0 0	6 0 0	76,800
600	Knights, - - - -	13	7,800	650 0	390,000	50 0	45 0 0	5 0 0	30,000
3,000	Esquires, - - - -	10	30,000	450 0	1,200,000	45 0	41 0 0	4 0 0	120,000
12,000	Gentlemen, - - - -	8	96,000	280 0	2,880,000	35 0	32 0 0	3 0 0	288,000
5,000	Persons in greater offices and places, - - - -	8	40,000	240 0	1,200,000	30 0	26 0 0	4 0 0	160,000
5,000	Persons in lesser offices and places, - - - -	6	30,000	120 0	600,000	20 0	17 0 0	3 0 0	90,000
2,000	Eminent merchants and traders by sea, - - -	8	16,000	400 0	800,000	50 0	37 0 0	13 0 0	208,000
8,000	Lesser merchants and traders by sea, - - -	6	48,000	198 0	1,600,000	53 0	27 0 0	6 0 0	288,000
10,000	Persons in the law, - - -	7	70,000	154 0	1,540,000	22 0	18 0 0	4 0 0	280,000
2,000	Eminent clergymen, - -	6	12,000	72 0	144,000	12 0	10 0 0	2 0 0	24,000
8,000	Lesser clergymen, - - -	5	40,000	50 0	400,000	10 0	9 4 0	0 16 0	32,000
40,000	Freeholders of the better sort,	7	280,000	91 0	3,640,000	13 0	11 15 0	1 5 0	350,000
120,000	Freeholders of the lesser sort,	5½	660,000	55 0	6,600,000	10 0	9 10 0	0 10 0	330,000
150,000	Farmers, - - - -	5	750,000	42 10	6,375,000	8 10	8 5 0	0 5 0	187,500
15,000	Persons in liberal arts and sciences, - - - -	5	75,000	60 0	900,000	12 0	11 0 0	1 0 0	75,000
50,000	Shopkeepers and tradesmen,	4½	225,000	45 0	2,250,000	10 0	9 0 0	1 0 0	225,000
60,000	Artisans and handicrafts, -	4	240,000	38 0	2,280,000	9 10	9 0 0	0 10 0	120,000
5,000	Naval officers, - - -	4	20,000	80 0	400,000	20 0	18 0 0	2 0 0	40,000
4,000	Military officers, - - -	4	16,000	60 0	240,000	15 0	14 0 0	1 0 0	16,000
500,586		5½	2,675,520	68 18	34,488,800	12 18	11 15 4	1 2 8 *Decrease*	3,023,700 *Decrease*
50,000	Common seamen, - - -	3	150,000	20 0	1,000,000	7 0	7 10 0	0 10 0	75,000
364,000	Labouring people and out-servants, - - - -	3½	1,275,000	15 0	5,460,000	4 10	4 12 0	0 2 0	127,500
400,000	Cottagers and paupers, - -	3¼	1,300,000	6 10	2,000,000	2 0	2 5 0	0 5 0	325,000
35,000	Common soliders, - - -	2	70,000	14 0	490,000	7 0	7 10 0	0 10 0	35,000
849,000		3¼	2,795,000	10 10	8,950,000	3 5	3 9 0	0 4 0	562,500
	Vagrants; as gipsies, thieves, beggars, etc., - - -		30,000		60,000	2 0	4 0 0	2 0 0	60,000
	So the general account is								
500,586	Increasing the wealth of the kingdom, - - - -	5½	2,675,520	68 18	34,488,800	12 18	11 15 4	1 2 8	3,023,700
849,000	Decreasing the wealth of the kingdom, - - - -	3½	2,825,000	10 10	9,010,000	3 3	3 7 6	0 4 0	622,500
1,349,586	Neat totals, - -	4¹⁄₁₅	5,500,520	32 5	43,491,800	7 18	7 9 3	0 8 9	2,401,200

England in 1986

A broad impression of the present distribution of the main farming systems

% Agricultural land use

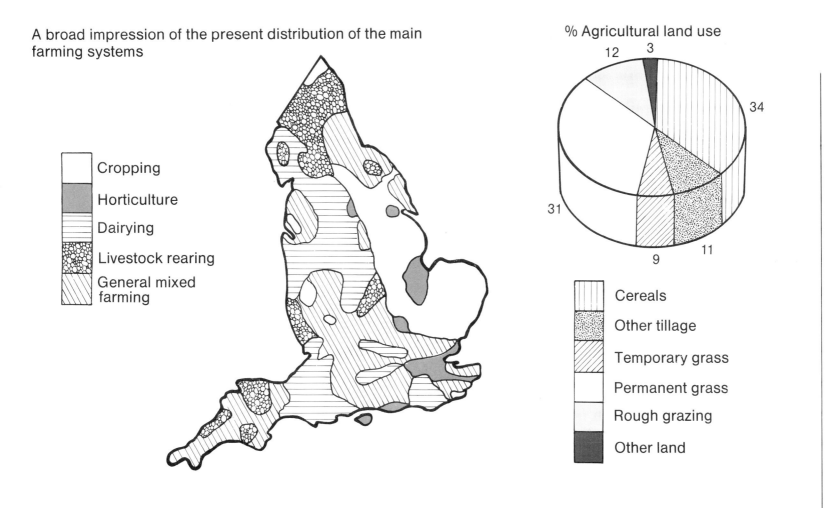

Legend (farming systems):
- Cropping
- Horticulture
- Dairying
- Livestock rearing
- General mixed farming

Legend (agricultural land use):
- Cereals
- Other tillage
- Temporary grass
- Permanent grass
- Rough grazing
- Other land

Pie chart values: 12, 3, 34, 11, 9, 31

Cornish Coast

Household food consumption 1980/85

Total annual consumption '000 tonnes

Number of minutes worked by the 'average' man to earn the price of food

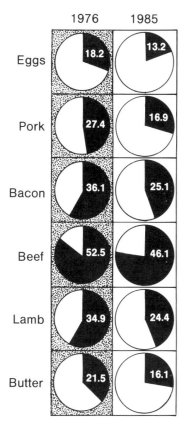

	1976	1985
Eggs	18.2	13.2
Pork	27.4	16.9
Bacon	36.1	25.1
Beef	52.5	46.1
Lamb	34.9	24.4
Butter	21.5	16.1

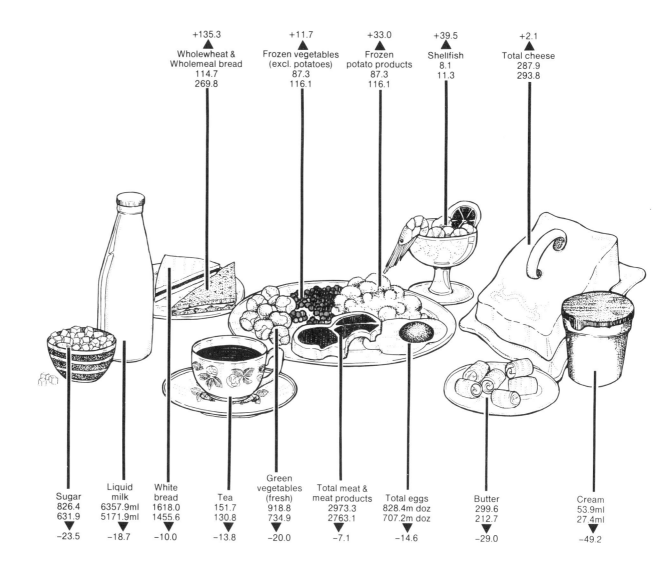

+135.3 ▲
Wholewheat &
Wholemeal bread
114.7
269.8

+11.7 ▲
Frozen vegetables
(excl. potatoes)
87.3
116.1

+33.0 ▲
Frozen
potato products
87.3
116.1

+39.5 ▲
Shellfish
8.1
11.3

+2.1 ▲
Total cheese
287.9
293.8

Sugar
826.4
631.9
▼
−23.5

Liquid
milk
6357.9ml
5171.9ml
▼
−18.7

White
bread
1618.0
1455.6
▼
−10.0

Tea
151.7
130.8
▼
−13.8

Green
vegetables
(fresh)
918.8
734.9
▼
−20.0

Total meat &
meat products
2973.3
2763.1
▼
−7.1

Total eggs
828.4m doz
707.2m doz
▼
−14.6

Butter
299.6
212.7
▼
−29.0

Cream
53.9ml
27.4ml
▼
−49.2

151

Ribblesdale Farm

Agricultural prices in England

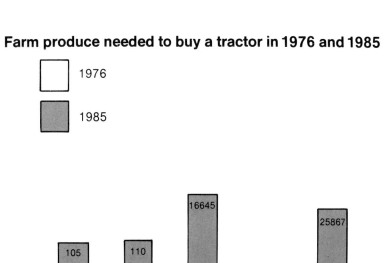

Farmgate prices

Farm input prices

Input prices excluding feedingstuffs

Index 1976 = 100

Year	Farmgate	Farm input	Input excl. feedingstuffs
1977	102.4	115.5	113.1
1979	115.3	131.7	134.9
1981	134.8	162.2	175.9
1983	152.9	185.8	201.5
1985	149.3	195.3	221.5

Farm produce needed to buy a tractor in 1976 and 1985

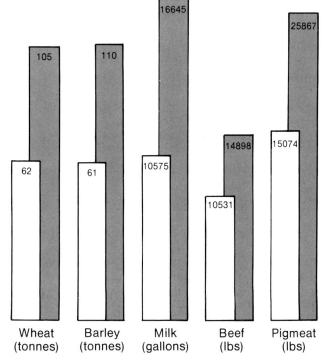

1976

1985

Produce	1976	1985
Wheat (tonnes)	62	105
Barley (tonnes)	61	110
Milk (gallons)	10575	16645
Beef (lbs)	10531	14898
Pigmeat (lbs)	15074	25867

153

Population Growth in England 1000-1990 AD (millions)

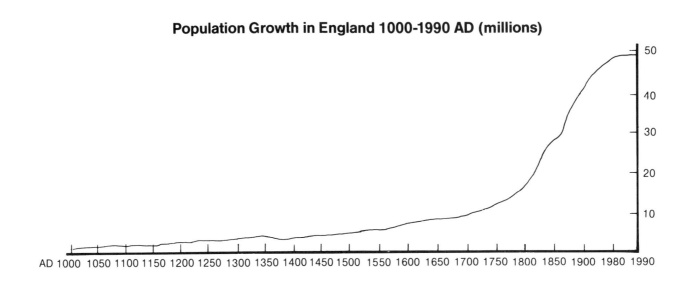

Employment in agriculture in England   Regular whole-time workers (thousands)

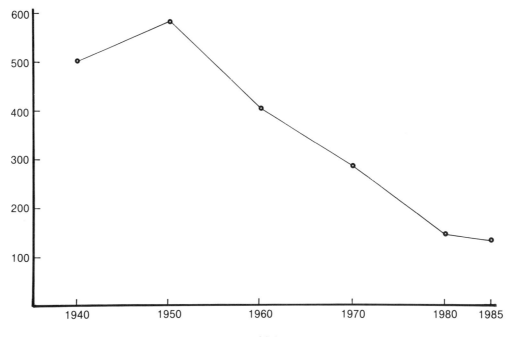

Real Farming Income*
Average 1973 – 1986 – 100

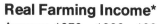 = Income Trend

* Deflated by the Retail Price Index

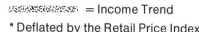

Use of inorganic fertilisers in England

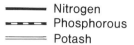
- Nitrogen
- Phosphorous
- Potash

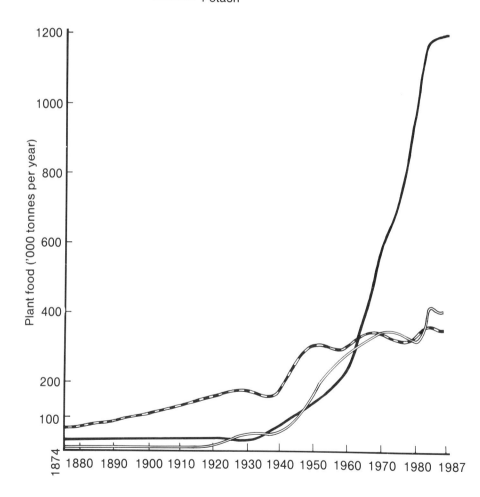

Plant food ('000 tonnes per year)

155

Dorset Farm